VEDA

Vedas mean....

Veda means *Jnana* or ultimate wisdom.

Yasya nisvasito Vedaha. Vedas are the very breath of Sarveswara, the Supreme Being. They are synonymous with God.

The Vedas are the foundation of our Sanatana Dharma and are the revelations of Eternal Truth. Our worship of the Supreme Being is through recitation and worship of the Vedas. Vedas are unique in that they offer a range of *Jnana* that covers the existent and nonexistent, the gross and the subtle, the past, the present, the future and beyond.

The Vedas have been preserved from time immemorial with phonetic exactitude, preservation of tonal accent and uncorrupted by any insertions.

Can there be anything more wondrous than this?

Sruti is another familiar name for the Vedas. *Sruti* means resonance, and the venerated Rishis were endowed with faculties to receive these divine vibrations and pass them down the ages by a process of precise phonetic recitation.

Learning was by listening, recitation & assimilation and *not* by recording or reading.

Each sound of the Vedas that was taught to the disciple had a specific tonal quality, called *swara*, and the teachings had to be learnt without blemish, by listening alone. Vedic mantras were passed on from generation to generation by our unique *Guru-sishya parampara* i.e., teacher-student relationship.

Thus over time the Vedas have been preserved in their pristine purity.

Some more names of Vedas

Aamnaaya and *Nigama* are two other names for the Vedas.

Aamnaaya: Aamnaaya has meanings like sacred, handed down by repetition.

Nigama: Nigama denotes the command that the teachings be followed in letter and spirit, with nothing left vague or susceptible to dilution.

The Vedas are also termed as *Apaurusheya*, i.e. not created by any agent. There are some more names for the Vedas like *Anushrava, Trayi, Brahma* etc.

Are Rishis the author of Vedas?

Vedas are *Apaurusheya* -- not created by a person, even a rishi. Had Rishis created them, they would have been called *Mantra-kartas.* Instead Rishis are called *Mantra-drashtaas* - they discovered the mantras, they perceived the Vedas through their superior wisdom. They listened and understood the ever-present Vedas and passed them on to posterity.

Vedas are the creation of the *Sarvagna* (omniscient) *Sarweswara* (the Supreme Lord) as per His own *sankalpa*, divine resolve. Eswara taught the Vedas first to Lord Brahma not through recitation but by His divine resolve. A detailed description of this could be had from a reading of Srimad Bhagavatam.

A modern-day analogy is transfer of data from one electronic device to another through wireless transmission.

After Brahma, *Prajapatis* standardized the transmission of the Vedas by a particular method known as *sandhai* and *thiruvai* that is prevalent even today in *Veda pathasalas*.

The Vedic language

Sanskrit, the most ancient of all languages, is the language of the Vedas. We have seen that they were born out of the *sankalpa* of Sarveswara. The Vedas are His very wisdom. Their language is His language.

While on the subject I would like to make a related observation. There is historical evidence to show that Tamil and Sanskrit have been in vogue from very ancient times. And like Sanskrit Tamil is independent of all other languages. Sanskrit is even more ancient than Tamil.

One would be able to infer this from the realization that the Vedas have their origin in ageless past, and were recited for the first time in Sanskrit. This alone is sufficient to indicate that Sanskrit is as old as the Vedas.

We are aware that most of the languages of the world have expanded and enriched themselves by freely borrowing words from other languages. But Vedic Sanskrit is complete in itself with specific grammar and prosody that have not changed with the times. Here we speak of the Sanskrit of the Vedas, which is different from the Sanskrit that later came to be used as a social language.

How old are the Vedas?

There have been numerous debates and "researches" on the age of Vedas, made both in our country and across the world. It is impossible to determine the exact age of the Vedas. However, we see that many scholars all over the world have assigned various age estimates. While linguistic experts put the Vedic period as

4,000 years old and the experts in Astronomy by and large concur, archeologists say it could be 5,000 years old. Some German scholars and archeologists including Prof. Maeterlinck say that the Vedic period could be at least a few lakh years old. In his well-known book, Satyartha Prakasam, Maharishi Dayananda asserts that if we consider that 6 manvantaras and 28 chaturyugas have passed by so far, the Vedas should have been in existence for at least 196,08,53,000 years! We can only say that all findings are inconsistent and are at best educated guesses.

Many Western scholars have done their 'research' on the Vedic period, but unlike other religious scriptures the Vedas themselves defy precise declaration of their age. No scholarly research can fix the period because the Vedas are beyond the most sophisticated methods of modern-day sciences.

Vedas are the very breath of Sarveswara. They have no origin that can be defined by man-made coordinates they are omnipresent.

The Vedas are divine.

The four Vedas

The Vedic statement *ananta vai Vedaha* means Vedas are infinite.

To illustrate this we have an interesting episode in *Kaataka Prasna* appearing in the Yajur Veda. With the blessing of Lord Indra, Sage Bharadwaja performed Veda *adhyayana* for three life spans. Pleased by this, Eswara appeared before him and granted him a boon. Sage Bharadwaja requested the Lord to grant him yet another lifespan so that he could complete *adhyayana* of the rest of the Vedas. Eswara smiled and showed him a mountain that comprised the Vedas, took three handfuls of soil from the mountain and told the Sage "this is all you have learnt so far". This was only to show the sheer magnitude of the Vedas and the near impossibility of mastering them even with all the time at one's command.

The Vedas are four in number. This may appear confusing when we regard the volume of the Vedas as infinite. The numbering of Vedas as four and the classification is by taking *lakshana* or characteristic and not *grantha* or the letter as the criterion. Sri Veda Vyasa classifies the Vedas into:

1. Rig Veda
2. Yajur Veda (Krishna & Shukla)
3. Sama Veda
4. Atharva Veda

Generally each Veda is a combination of the following groups of texts:

1. Samhitai
2. Braahmana
3. Aaranyaka
4. Upanishads

1. *Samhitai* is the mantra portion of the Vedas, and is considered as the main text of the Vedas.

2. *Braahmana* is elucidation of the practices and main mantras. It classifies the Vedic rituals and duties, and delineates the methods of performing them.

3. *Aaranyaka* offers deeper meaning and gives the philosophy of the first two parts.

4. Upanishads form the part of *Jnana Kanda*. These give *marga* or guidance for those seeking liberation and salvation. Upanishads are philosophical in nature.

   While there is some difference of opinion on the exact number of Upanishads, 10 of them, listed below, are considered very important as they have bhasyas of Sankara, the earliest commentaries available. The names of these 10 Upanishads and the Vedas to which they belong are given hereunder:

Name of the Veda	Name of the Upanishad
Rig Veda	Aitareya Upanishad
Krishna Yajur Veda	Taittiriya Upanishad • Kathopanishad
Shukla Yajur Veda	Isa Upanishad Brahadaranyaka Upanishad
Sama Veda	Kena Upanishad Chandogya Upanishad
Atharva Veda	Mundaka Upanishad Prashna Upanishad Mandukya Upanishad

• Here some add Maha Narayana Upanishad also.

Of the many many branches of the four Vedas we have at present only 10 branches in practice. Even among these 10 branches, the painful truth is that only 7 branches are actively taught in pathashalas throughout India. The reality is even more depressing: the study of the Vedas is on the wane.

The question that arises and must be answered is: what is the role, in preserving the Vedas, of those born as Brahmins and entrusted with the propagation of knowledge?

Vedas and God

All Vedas solemnly affirm: *Sarve Vedaha yatraikam bhavanti* (Taittiriya Aaranyaka) i.e., all the Vedas meet and mingle in the Lord. And hence it becomes clear that Vedas and God are not different.

The Vedas declare that it does not matter if you see the God in one form or another, and worship Him in one way or another. You can still reach Him and realize the Ultimate Truth, the Supreme Being. Can you find this all-encompassing sentiment in any other religious literature?

Vedas, being knowledge, cannot be comprehended in full. With all the guidance from our elders and with the Grace of God, we are blessed with its grandeour and the essence and import of them.

Are Vedas and Vedanta the same?

The quintessence of the Vedas may be called Vedanta. Vedanta is all philosophy. The *Brahma Sutra* and Upanishads deal with Vedanta. A detailed study of the real character of Brahma and the import of the Vedas are explained in the Vedanta.

Those of us who are beset with day-to-day living need not worry too much about Vedantic concepts. We may first bring into practice the religious duties stipulated in the Vedas with the initiation of a Guru. With consistent and regular practice of *our Karmas*, the concepts of Vedanta will start revealing itself slowly.

Vedanga - the six limbs

It is incorrect to try and interpret Vedas with our current knowledge of the Sanskrit language, which is quite different from Vedic Sanskrit. The two languages may agree on some fundamentals but they are not the same. Only a person who is thorough with the six *angas* of Vedas described below should venture to give commentaries on Veda Mantras.

The six angas are: *siksha, kalpa, vyakarana, nirukta, chandas and jyotisha.*

Siksha: swara, akshara and matra -- these are the basics and this part ensures that the practitioner pronounces the words exactly.

Kalpa: This part is intended to explain which mantras are to be used on which occasions, and how. This part, known as *prayoga*, is invaluable for the correct observance of the karmas.

Vyakarana: This part seeks to give meanings of the mantras. With mastery of this part we can start appreciating the inner meaning of the Vedas.

Nirukta: This part establishes the correctness of the various namas used in Vedas. The main thrust here is the sense of sound.

Chandas: This part tells us about the characteristics of the words and letters that are used in the Vedas.

Jyotisha: This part is related to the determination of time and is mainly based on tejas. Also, this includes the science of astronomy.

The study and mastery of the six angas wil itself take many years. We can then try to study interpretations called *Bashyas*.

Thus, to understand the real import of the Vedas, our present knowledge of Sanskrit is grossly insufficient and needs to be taken to a significantly higher plane.

Veda Lakshana

How have the Vedas been handed down to us for ages together without any distortion?

In order to correctly recite the Vedas a practice called *vikruti* has been rigorously followed through the ages. This is made possible by adhering to the order and getting the words and intonation correctly as required. This practice has been made part and parcel of the learning process.

The book *Vikrutivalli* speaks of eight types of chanting of Vedas and getting them by heart. These are *jata, mala, sika, leka, dwaja, dhanda, ratha and ghanam.* Up to the level of krama, the Vedas are recited without change but after this stage is attained the student embarks on the practice of fine-tuning through the medium of *vikruti*. Our ancestors have ensured the correct pronunciation, intonation and use of words by the diligent and unswerving practice of the above eight ways. Thus the Vedas have continued to be recited without change of even a letter or note for a millennium and more.

It is no easy matter to reach up to the level of *Ghananta*; in fact, it is possible only with a firm resolve and tremendous practice. To reach the level of *Ghananta*, it will usually take more than one decade of full-time *adhyayana* or practice. Hence Veda *adhyayana* has to be started at an early age. It is heartening indeed to see students emerging in great numbers out of the portals of the Veda Pathashalas after mastering up to the level of *Ghana* in Rig and Yajur Vedas. Those who have completed up to the level of *Ghananta* are called *Ghanapathi* or *Ghanapaadigal*.

This particular way of chanting Veda mantras known as *Ghana-parayana*, that is mantras repeated in set patterns, is not only pleasant to hear but sends divine vibrations around and is very powerful. It also serves the purpose of preventing mistakes or unseemly changes from the original script.

About interpretation

We have several Bashyakars, great geniuses who have offered interpretation of the Vedas. A few names such as Bhatta Bhaskara, Uvata, Mahidhar, Venkata Madhava, Sayanacharya come to mind. Present day scholars going through these interpretations are so awed that they say the Bashyakars would not have been ordinary mortals.

While we stand in awe of the richness and depth of the Vedas the thought does arise: What should we do to make ourselves worthy, really deserving, of this wonderful treasure?

The recitation process

The *varna, swara and matra* are to be recited in the Vedas without blemish. Praati sakhya, a Sastra, has coded these aspects into a rigour. Even in day-to-day life we flinch when words are mispronounced or used badly. When that is so, can anyone imagine reciting Vedas with impure intonation or wrong accent? It is therefore vital that one should recite Veda mantras only with proper guidance from a Guru.

In this context, a new trend is the use of cassettes and CDs for learning Vedas. Out of their enthusiasm many try to learn by listening to recorded devices. Nothing can be more injurious: learning of Vedas should be only from a Guru.

Mechanical devices cannot correct mistakes that one is sure to make initally without being even aware of the mistake, and these will therefore become permanent.

It is equally incorrect for a student of the Vedas to be flippant in the memorising or pronunciation of the words. These have deep meaning and even deeper vibratory effects, and should not be taken casually.

Answering a question from Saunaka, Sage Kapila in Kapilasmriti has this to say: "One who wrongly recites the Vedas is a sinner: this is a sin worse than the three eternal sins of *brahmahatya, brunahatya* and *veerahatya*. A person who changes the words of the Vedas at his own free will is a sinner too."

Vedas and Science

Many of us are often seized with a doubt: do Vedas reflect scientific knowledge? Can Vedic pronouncements be proved scientifically?

I firmly believe, as also the traditionalists, that Vedas are meant for spiritual practice only and are not to be evaluated with reference to modern science.

I say this because Vedas are far beyond our thinking and imagination, far too vast for human comprehension. Why are we then trying to bring it down to modern science, which is at best ephemeral knowledge? The findings and recordings of modern science and technology are always susceptible to alteration. The progress is ongoing and never final. A scientific theory said to be valid at a given point of time is quite often rejected or modified after some time. Thus we cannot be sure of the correctness and perfection of scientific theories and facts. On the contrary, the knowledge embedded in Vedas is eternally valid and permanent - it has seen no change, and will see no change.

The interpretation of Vedas should be carried out with *aadhyatmika* or spiritual orientation. It does not lend itself to scientific analysis. People interested in search of scientific aspects in Vedas stretch the meanings of Vedic Mantras with great difficulty to fit modern research findings to them. The intentions of such scholars are good but I would submit that their work is like carrying a candle to the Sun. Many such analysts, despite proficiency in Sanskrit, chant mantras with a lot of distortion and do not know the significance of Vedic words. One should not attempt to interpret the Vedas unless one has thoroughly studied Vedanga, Sastras, Darshanas, Itihasas and Puranas. One should besides have a fair command over the Vedic commentaries of Sri Sayanacharya.

That said, we need not ignore the work of modern scholars, both Western and Indian, which try to prove that several branches of science are traced to Vedas. These research studies, which establish close ties between the Vedas on the one hand and modern sciences from Mathematics to Medicine to Computers and Cosmology, are very interesting and satisfy our modern mind. Let us not undermine the hard work and enthusiasm of these scholars. But let us also remember the eternal truth that the Vedas cannot be commented upon from a scientific point of view. Vedas are divine. God's work cannot be interpreted by the sciences created by man.

Edison, Max Muller and the Gramophone:

Many Western scholars, it can be said with authority, have spent several years sincerely understanding Vedas. It is also a fact that they learnt Sanskrit with this sole purpose and mastered the language. Many of them have also come out with very interesting positive theses on Vedas. Of course, the traditionalist may not agree with their commentaries completely but the sincere efforts of these scholars must be appreciated. The following evidence is a case in point, which readers are sure to find very interesting.

HMV had once published a pamphlet giving the history of gramophone record. When Thomas Alva Edison invented the gramophone record, which could record human voice for posterity, he wanted to record the voice of an eminent scholar on his first piece. He chose Prof. Max Muller of England, another great personality of the 19th century, for this purpose. He requested Max Muller to lend his voice at a public gathering. Max Muller was happy to acept, and spoke into the gramophone as guided by Edison.

When Edison played the gramophone disc, the audience was thrilled to hear the voice of Max Muller from the instrument.

It was then that Max Muller asked:"Did you understand what I said in the morning or what you heard in the afternoon?" The audience fell silent because they had not understood the language in which Max Muller had spoken. Max Muller then explained that the language he spoke was Sanskrit and it was the first sloka of Rig Veda, which says "Agni Meele Purohitam." This was the first recorded public version on the gramophone plate.

Why did Max Muller choose this sloka? Addressing the audience he said, "Vedas are the oldest text of the human race. And "Agni Meele Purohitam" is the first verse of Rig Veda. India has given to the world universal philosophies in the form of the Vedas."

(The full text of this event appears in 'Maxmuller and His Contemporaries' by Swami Prabhavananda, The Ramakrishna Mission Institute of Culture, Kolkatta-700 029. India)

Vedic grandeur

It is impossible to express in words the greatness of the Vedas.

Many conversations are found in Puranas between great souls, which throw light on the greatness of the Vedas. What follows is the gist of some legendary conversations (Courtesy:Navalpakkam Sri Kannan's Vedavaibhavam)between:

- Sage Yagyavalkya & King Janaka
- God Indra & Sage Bharadwaja
- Minister Malyavan & King Ravana
- Pandava brothers Nakula & Yudhishtra
- Sage Vasishta & King Yudhishtra
- Dharmaputra & Yaksha
- Pitamaha Bhishma & King Yudhishtra
- Lord Krishna & Arjuna
- Sage Parasurama & Bhishma
- Pitrus & Sage Parasurama

1. The path shown by Vedas should not be transgressed.
2. The performance of japa as enjoined by Vedas wipes out even great sins.
3. Veda Parayana is a form of nishkruti - work of unparalleled greatness.
4. The words of a person who has done Veda *abhyasa* have strength and stamina.
5. A place where Veda Parayana is conducted becomes holy.
6. It is not easy to practice Vedic chanting. It requires purity and attention to detail.
7. If we discontinue Vedic chanting, we are the losers; not the Vedas.

8. Vedic Mantras possess great power.

9. All who are connected with Veda Parayana - the persons who organise it, the persons who chant, the people who support, even the people who listen -- are blessed.

10. Doing Vedic chanting with rigour is equivalent to doing tapas.

11. Where there is the sound of Vedas there is no room for destitution.

12. To give one's daughter in marriage to a Vedic scholar is a great blessing.

13. Vedas and God are not different.

14. Vedas are permanent; they have no ruin.

15. Chanting of Vedas is the only way to ensure growth of Brahmanya.

16. The presence of Brahmins alone is not enough: it should be accompanied by the sound of Vedas being chanted (Veda ghosha).

17. The Vedas recognise and approve both *Grahasthashrama* and *Sanyasashrama*.

18. Only with the help of the Vedas can we perform our duties towards the Devas and our pitrus.

19. Vedas benefit not just a section of the society, it is for all humanity.

20. Idol worship, Bhakti marga (the path of devotion) and yoga marga (the path of penance) -- none of these is a contravention of Veda marga, or the path shown by the Vedas.

21. Vedas are the very embodiment of God. The words should be chanted with perfect sruti unison and clarity of diction.

22. We must invite only persons who have done Veda *adhyayana* to take part in a sraaddha.

    [Interestingly, this particular sentiment is expressed in the conversation between the Yaksha and Yudhishtra, an important section of the Mahabharata, which follows.]

    Questions the Yaksha:

    "Sraaddham mrutam gatam vaa syaat?" i.e., when does a Sraaddha lose its benefits and become infructuous?

    Answers Yudhishtra:

    "Mrutam asrotriyam sraaddham" i.e., when no Brahmin (as *Bhokta*) with Vedic knowledge takes part in the sraaddha it becomes futile.

23. When Vedas are ignored, the essence of Brahmanyam is gone: there will be nothing left.

24. Sri Hayagriva Bhagawan is still doing Veda Parayana as His Avatara is yet to be finished.

Some 'commandments' in the Vedas

From the omnipresent Vedas we derive many invaluable directions and guidelines, which are authoritative in nature.

- Behave in such a way that Lord loves you. That is more important than your loving Him *(Taittireya Samhita)*
- Don't be a debtor. *(Acchidram, Taittireya Samhita)*
- Be firm as a rock. *(Ekagni kandam)*
- Treat Brahmanas on par with Devas. *(1st kanda; Taittireya Samhita)*
- During the *monthly periods* of women keep away from them *(5th kanda, Taittireya Samhita)*
- Give your wife the right status and treat her with esteem. *(Ashtakam, Braahmanam)*

- Do not get upset over abuse heaped on you by someone. In fact their abuse indirectly helps you, because in a sense it is absolution of your past karma. You should learn to welcome it *(2nd Ashtakam, Braahmanam)*
- If you have to receive dana (get a donation), receive it only from a deserving person who has got it by the right means. *(1st Ashtakam, Braahmanam)*
- Speak only good words. *(Aranyaka)*
- Do not criticise the food you take. Do not waste food. And cook food in abundant quantities so you will never have to refuse a mendicant. *(Bruguvalli Upanishad,Yajur Veda)* [the Veda adds *"tad vratam"* - i.e., make this a firm resolve.]
- Learning is possible only for the awake, the alert and the conscious.
- Diligently follow the path of the ancestors and you shall achieve greatness.
- Do not slacken when performing good deeds.
- To realize God, hear only about Him; think only about Him; and meditate only on Him.

Some precious edicts from the Vedas that give us useful advice on leading the good life:

- Direct your efforts first on acquiring knowledge of the Vedas before seeking any other learning.
- Do not drink. Do not make drunkards your acquaintances.
- Do not waste time looking for reasons to learn the Vedas. You do not need any motives for Veda *adhyayana*. It is your duty, no less.
- Avoid words of negativity.

- Memorize the Vedas and internalize the knowledge.
- Learn Vedas only from a Guru.
- Never allow more than three successive generations in your family to miss the study of the Vedas.
- Learning and teaching Vedas is a form of intense worship.

****

OUR REVERED MAHARISHIS

Elsewhere we have seen that Maharishis are the discoverers of Vedas. And that is why they are called *mantra drashta*. Because of their supreme eminence, they are called Maharishis. Despite their calibre that was no less than that of the Devas, they are treated as humans since they lived among human beings on earth. It is impossible not to be awestruck by their *jnana*, spirit of sacrifice, simplicity and the invaluable service they have rendered to the world. That we are descendants of those great men is a great honour in itself. Verily we are fortunate.

Maharishis belong to different groups variously called Brahma Rishis, Raja Rishis, etc. They are *jnanis* spanning across the past, present and future. They are omnipresent, omniscient and omnipotent.

There are countless Maharishis - some visible and others invisible. We will now acquaint you with a few of these great men and what they have done for us. (Courtesy: Veda Vignanam)

Kasyapa:

Sage Kasyapa is credited with the creation of Surya Bhagawan (Sun God). Mahavishnu who was born to him and Aditi. Here is a Maharishi who was the father of Bhagawan himself.

Atri:

Sage Atri finds a mention in Rig Veda. Once upon a time, the two illuminators of the world, Surya and Chandra, were wounded and hence the light that they showered on the world diminished. Sage Atri, with the Vedic prowess that he possessed, substituted for them and ensured brightness of the world. At the request of the Devas he restored the position of Surya and Chandra.

Vasistha:

Sage Vasistha was born as per the divine wish of Lord Brahma. He was incomparable in his ability to conquer lust and anger. It is said that the essence of Devas -- Mitra and Varuna -- appeared as divine light and fell into a pot and Vasistha was born out of it. Arundhati, the personification of virtue and chastity, was his spouse. We find the description of Vasistha's power of penance (*tapobala*) in Srimad Ramayana.

Viswamitra:

The divine powers of Sage Viswamitra are beyond words. He is a standing example, a great model, for never-say-die attitude, and for persistence in achieving the goal in the face of insurmountable obstacles. He strained himself to the maximum and got the title Brahma Rishi from no less a person than Sage Vasistha. His *tapobala* was so immense that he could send Trisanku to heaven while still in the human form, the body intact. He was also instrumental to the marriage of Lord Rama with Sita.

Jamadagni:

Sage Jamadagni, so-called because he shines as bright as Agni (fire), was Sage Viswamitra's sister's son. Renuka Devi, his wife, is legendary for her chastity, and is worshipped as Mahamayi or Mariamman in Tamil Nadu. Parasurama was one of their many sons. Jamadagni continues to reside in the *sapta-rishi* mandala.

Gautama:

It is said that Gautama was a master's master in the Vedas. Ahalya, his wife, was the daughter born out of the divine will of Lord Brahma. Brahma Purana says that it was Sage Gautama who created the river Godavari by his penance. For this reason the river is also known as Gautami.

Bharadwaja:

Waja means food. Sage Bharadwaja gave great prominence to Annadana (donating food) and probably earned the name Bharadwaja as a result. He was born out of the divine will of Brahaspati. He was a great expert in Vedas. His Ashram was a byword for receiving guests and entertaining them to extraordinary levels of delight. There are many legends associated with his Vedic powers and his insatiable quest for the knowledge of the Vedas.

Agastya:

Sage Agastya worshipped Sri Rama, and when the Lord came to his hermitage, the Sage deemed it the fruits of his penance. His wife was Lopamudra. There are many episodes to show his unbelievable achievements. He drank the ocean just by *achamana.* He vanquished the demon Vatapi. The height of Vindhya mountains was curtailed by him. He is said to have codified the grammar for Tamil language.

Brugu:

Brugu Rishi is yet another creation out of the divine will of Lord Brahma. He was an embodiment of penance. Sage Markandeya was the grandson of this Rishi. In yet another janma (life), he did strenuous penance completely unmindful of his own existence and white ants built an anthill over him, giving him the name Valmiki. Goddess Mahalakshmi herself acquiesced to become his daughter. He is thus called Srivatsa. The Srivatsa Gotra is named after this sage. As Goddess Mahalakshmi married Mahavishnu, this Rishi naturally was the father-in-law of the Lord Himself - what an honour!

Markandeya:

Destiny ordained that Markandeya would die at the age of 16. His parents Sage Mrugandu and Marutvati were plunged in sorrow, and to relieve them of their suffering he did strenuous penance on Lord Siva and got a boon to be among the chiranjeevis – immortals. He spread the knowledge of various Puranas throughout his life and pleased with his service to the lore, Lord Siva bestowed on him the title Puranacharya.

Sanatkumara:

Sage Sanatkumara is always referred to along with his three brothers - Sanaka, Sanandana, and Sanaatana. They were all born out of the divine will of Lord Brahma. Sage Narada was the disciple of Sage Sanatkumara.

Narada:

Narada was the creation of Lord Brahma. Instead of taking the difficult path of penance, he took to reciting forever the sweet name of Hari, called Harikeertana. He was always seen with the Veena in his hands, effortlessly going around the worlds uttering Hari's holy name. He was equally at home with the Asuras (demons). He was a master of the four Vedas, the six Sastras and the sixty-four arts. He was instrumental in getting the divine grace of the Lord bestowed on Druva and Prahlada who were mere children - their age did not matter to Narada.

Vyasa:

Vyasa was the son of Sri Parasara, the great *Jnani*. He was born to Satyavati, also known as Matsyagandhi. Sage Vyasa was known in his early years as Krishna Dvaipayana. Sri Parasurama performed his Upanayana and taught him Vedas, which was then not manualised and notated for effective dissemination. Sage Vyasa classified and codified Vedas into the four segments we see today. He taught Rig, Yajur, Sama and Atharva Vedas to Sages Paila, Vaisampayana, Jaimini and Sumantu respectively. Another priceless treasure he gave mankind is the epic Mahabharata. Sage Suka was his son. It was given to Suka to preach the Srimad Bhagavatam, again composed by Sage Vyasa, to king Parikshit. Vyasa is said to have written the 18 puranas.

Dadhichi:

Dadhichi Rishi is the very epitome of sacrifice for the welfare of others. For the destruction of the demon Vrtrasura Lord Indra requested him to give his backbone and Sage Dadhichi gave his backbone instantly, at the cost of his very life, for this cause. It is said that he did strenuous penance in the Naimisaranya forest.

Brihaspati:

Sage Brihaspati is the Devas' Guru. As he is the leader of several teams - Brahmanaganas, Devaganas and Kaviganas - he is also called Ganapati, Brahmanaspathi and Jyeshtharajan. The well-known mantra starting "*Gananaam tva Ganapatigm havamahe*" pertains to Sage Brihaspati. This mantra came to be used in subsequent times for worshipping Lord Ganapati. Brihaspati remains unparalleled in sharpness of mind and knowledge of the Sastras. Devas attribute their welfare entirely to his sage advice.

Gargacharya:

Gargacharya was an expert in the art of Jyotisha (astrology as well as astronomy). It is learnt that this great Sage performed the Namakarana of Lord Krishna. Sage Pranadharta was his son.

The foregoing is by no means an exhaustive list of the Maharishis: these are just a few of the great souls. What you have read of them again is a miniscule part of their achievements. You will find it an absorbing and a rewarding pursuit, if you read more about them and other Rishis.

SUTRAKARA RISHIS

These Sutrakars also come under the category of Rishis. There are many branches of each Veda. We have to perform the *Srauta* and *Smarta* karmas based on the branch to which we belong. The Rishis who have endowed us with the *poorva* and *apara* prayogas, i.e. the manuals according to which we have to perform rituals for the living and for the departed, are known as Sutrakars.

Their names are:

Aapasthamba

Bodhayana

Bharadwaja

Satyashadha

Vikhanasa

Aswalayana

Kausheetaka

Katyayana

Drahyayana

Jaimini

Kausika

There are other names as well.

One interesting note here - Sri Adi Sankara describes Aapasthamba as Bhagawan Aapasthamba. This is greatness indeed!

One more point about these great Rishis. *Sanyasashrama* is not compulsory for being a Rishi. They led the life of a grahasta and yet obtained the grace of God and guided the society practising the grihastashrama dharma.They were fully involved in following Vedic practices like Yaga-yajna and rituals associated with Agni and still lived enviable lives full of Vedic achievements.

One can get names of more Maharishis from the list of the *Gotra-pravara* also. This is when one says *abhivadana* to elders, in the course of which Rishis' names are uttered depending upon one's Gotra.

Our lineage is from Maharishis

Each of us belongs to a "Gotra". Everyone one of these Gotras is associated with some Maharishis. When we introduce ourselves through *"abhivadaye"* after performing namaskara, we invoke the names of the Rishis associated with our Gotras.

The list of different Gotras and the associated Rishis follows::

Gotras and releted Rishis

Here is a table containging some of the Gotras with names of Pravara Rishis

GOTRA	PRAVARA RISHIS
Srivatsa	Bharghava, Chyavana, Aapnavana, Aurva, Jaamadagnya
Bharadhwaja	Angirasa, Baarhaspatya, Bharadhwaja
Shadamarshana	Angirasa, Paurukutsya, Thrasadasya
Atreya	Atreya, Aarchanaanasa, Syavaasva
Vadhula	Bharghava, Vaitahavya, Saavedasa
Kausika Kausika	Vaisavamitra, Aghamarshana,
Viswamitra	Vaisvamitra, Dhaivaratha, Authala
Kaundinya	Vaasishta, Maitravaruna, Kaudinya
Harita	a. Angirasa, Ambareesha, Yauvanaasva b. Harita, Ambareesha,Yauvanaasva
Maudgalya	a. Angirasa, Baarmyasva, Maudkalya b. Tharkshaya, Baarmyasva, Maudkalya c. Angirasa, Taavya, Maudgalya
Sandilya	a. Kasyapa, Avatsara, Sandilya b. Kasyapa, Avatsara, Daivala c. Kasyapa, Daivala, Asitha
Kasyapa	Kasyapa, Avatsara, Naidhruva
Kutsa	Angirasa, Maantra, Kautsa
Kaanva	a. Angirasa, Aaajaameeda, Kaanva b. Angirasa, Kaura, Kaanva
Paraasara	Vaasishta, Saaktya, Paaraasarya

Agastya	Aagastya, Taardyasyuta, Saumavaha
Garga	a. Angirasa, Barhaspatya, Bharadhwaja, Sainya, Gargya b. Angirasa, Sainya, Gargya
Badarayana	Angirasa, Barshatasva, Raatheetara
Sankruthi	a. Angirasa, Kauraveeta, Saankrutya b. Saatya, Kauraveeta, Saankrutya
Arshtishena	Bharghava, Chyavana, Apnavana, Aarshishena, Aanupa
Kapi	Angirasa, Aamahaiya, Orukshaya
Kapila	Angirasa, Aamahaiya, Orukshaya
Mitrayuva	Bharghava, Vaatryasva, Daivodasa
Vainya	Bharghava, Vainya, Paarta
Kanaka	Saunaka (or) Grutsamata
Gautama	Angirasa, Aayaasya, Gautama
Garga	Gargya, Kaustubha, Mandavya
Kaatyaayana	Atreya, Bharghava, Vaasishta
Sandilya	Sandilya, Asita, Daivala
Saavarna	Aurva, Chyavana, Bharghava, Jamadagnya, Apnavana
Sakthi	Saakta, Paaraasara, Vaasishta
Kaanvaayana	Kaanvaayana, Angirasa, Barhaspatya, Bhaaradwaja, Ajaameeda
Bruhaspati	Barhaspatya, Kaapila, Baarvana
Kaakshivanta	Angirasa, Ausatya, Kaaksheevantha, Gautama, Kamanta
Aayasya	Angirasa, Aayaasya, Gautama

NB: There could be some variations in the sequence of Rishis. For exact pronunciations of the names please consult elders.

IMPORTANCE OF KUSHMANDA HOMA

-the homa found in the Vedas-

We may classify *homas* into two broad categories.

One may be classified as *Kaamyartha* homa, to derive gain and fulfill certain wishes. The other one is *Prayaschitta* homa, to deliver us of the sins of our undesirable acts of omission and commission. *Kushmanda homa* falls in the second category.

Difference between Yaga and Homa: *Yaga* and *Homa* are not the same. Yagas are categorized as 'srauta' karmas and are performed in 'agnihotra' agnis. Homas are categorized as 'smarta' karmas and are performed in 'aupasana' agni.

Agnihotra Agni: This Agni has the characteristic of being a continuum. Yaga is performed by highly qualified Vedic scholars, who have to be Grahastas, well-versed in all the prayogas and Sastras as well, for universal benefit. Yagas such as Aswamedha, Soma and Vajapeya come under this category. Vedas speak about Yagas, which come under the category of 'Srauta karmas'.

Aupasana Agni: All Grahastas (married persons) have to perform *Aupasana* every day both in the morning and in the evening. Homas like Vastu and Sraaddha are done in *Aupasana Agni*.

A few more examples of homas would be the Ganapati homa, Navagraha homa and Sudarshana homa which are done in *laukika agni. These homas are referred to as 'Smarta karmas'.*

Homas have been codified, compiled and given to us by Sages with their divine powers.

While the Vedas speak about Yagas, they contain no reference to homas - with the exception of one homa, i.e. *Kushmanda Homa.*

The details of this powerful homa are found in the Yajur Veda (Second *prasnam* in *Taitreeya Aaranyaka*)

Why is it done?

The great Sengalipuram Anantarama Diskshitar has this to say:

"...Further, this homa can be performed as a prelude to auspicious events (mangala karya) like Upanayana, Vivaha, etc. It gives one the confidence and qualification for the mangala karya. It is also the practice of some to observe this homa prior to doing the annual Pratyabdika Sraaddha.

Likewise, a person wishing to cleanse himself of a sin he may have unwiittingly committed, does this homa and gets cleared. Such is the power of Kushmanda Homa."

The mantras in Kushmanda homa speak of certain sins people commit, and specifically clears them of the ill-effects of these sins upon doing the homa. Some of the sins referred to are:

1. Being casual or arrogant in Deva karmas
2. Lying in the course of day to day activities
3. Speaking ill of others
4. The hardship we cause to our mother during our presence in her *garbha*.
5. The mental anguish we cause to our parents with or without our knowledge.
6. Bad behaviour
7. Using impolite language while speaking to our elders, Purohits or Acharyas.

The mantras also clarify benefits that can accrue to the person doing Kushmanda homa. Some of the benefits:

- If one has got into unmanageable debts, the homa helps to raise one's status and return the debts in one's own lifetime.

- There are mantras that will give us sound health and a pure heart and make us better human beings.

- Crossing the sea -- the only method of foreign travel in olden days -- was considered a sin, and even today some sticklers for ritual perform kushmanda homa after they return, to cleanse themselves.

How is Kushmanda Homa to be performed?

Kushmanda homa is surprisingly simple in terms of the process, and therefore it does not cost much. The number of Ritviks (Purohits) required is minimal. Apart from the *Pradhana* Acharya, one or two scholars are enough.

Of course one can invite more Purohits if one wishes to do the homa on a larger scale. Even the Homa *dravyam*, articles used for Homa, are very few.

While the material aspects of the homa are easy to observe, the rigours -- niyamas -- that have to be followed are quite stiff and demanding.

The following aspects have been codified and have to be observed with total diligence and faith:

1) *Diksha niyama* (Ritualistic discipline)
(at least for a fortnight)

2) Gayatri japa to the maximum extent
(a minimum of 1,008 per day for the fortnight)

3) A ritualistic bath in line with the advice of the Purohit on the day of the homa

4) Naandi Sraaddha
(this is not needed when the Kushmanda homa is done as a prelude to *Pratyabdika Sraaddha*)

No '*Power of Attorney*':

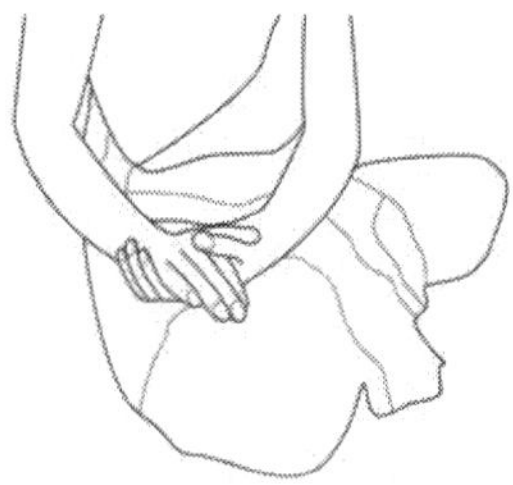

There is one more unique feature in the performance of this homa. In most homas, the usual practice is after the *Sankalpa*, the Purohit receives the 'Power of Attorney' from the Karta and does the actual job, with the help of other Purohits present, with the karta a mute spectator.

In Kushmanda homa, the karta has to personally perform the Homa in his *Aupasana Agni* under the guidance of the Sastrigal, and chant all the mantras himself.

In summary, this homa is one of immense significance and has great value. It is a great remedy for absolution of a person's conscious and unconscious sins, if done with devotion and in complete consonance with the laid down procedure.

The benefits that accrue from Kushmanda homa are many - the most important of which is peace of mind.

****

MAHABHARATA

Over time, Mahabharata has come to be termed as the *fifth Veda*; it is replete with many fascinating, comprehensive intricacies of Dharma Sastras.

Even though it is one among the *puranas*, it occupies special status because of its eminence. It has been raised to the status of *Itihasa* along with Srimad Ramayana.

It is important that we study the epic *parva-wise.* There are 18 parvas. They are:

1. Adi Parva	10. Sauptika Parva
2. Sabha Parva	11. Stri Parva
3. Vana Parva	12. Shanti Parva
4. Virata Parva	13. Anushasana Parva
5. Udyoga Parva	14. Ashvamedhika Parva
6. Bhishma Parva	15. Ashramavasika Parva
7. Drona Parva	16. Mausala Parva
8. Karna Parva	17. Mahaprasthanika Parva
9. Shalya Parva	18. Svargarohana Parva

While many have written treatises on Mahabarata, at best they have created awareness of the Itihasa, since their writings are not written parva-wise, in full.

A full printout of Mahabharata in 18 parvas may go to 5,000 pages. Only if we read the entire book can we get a glimpse of its power and savour the originality.

The conversation between Sri Yudhishtra and Sri Krishna Paramatma on *Braahmanyam* would be worth a glance here.This is contained in the 96th and 97th chapters of the *Aswamedika Parva*- one out of the eighteen parvas.

Asks Yudhishtra: Kesava! Janardhana! Who is a Brahmin? What is his true character?

Sri Krishna: Listen to Me, Oh, Yudhishtra! Great one among the ardent followers of dharma! It is they

- who have tuft, who wear Yajyopaveeta,
- who worship Agni,
- who love their spouse,
- who recite Vedas,
- who worship Devi Gayatri through performing Sandhyavandana
- who perform their duties towards guests and
- who perform *pitru karmas* with devotion...

Oh King, Pandava, listen to me further. Even if one were to be a Brahmin by birth and were to be highly accomplished, I will consider their life a mere waste if they

- do not perform Deva karmas,
- are greedy,
- have no love for their spouse,
- discriminate while serving food,
- show disrespect to their mother, father or Guru
- do not perform Sandhyavandana,
- do not respect the words of father-in-law and mother-in-law,
- earn their living by usury,
- are impostors
- and neglect their nitya karmas

Mahabharata also has the following two episodes known as Yaksha Prasna and Bhishma's upadesa (advice).

Yaksha prasna

One day, during their exile of Pandavas, a deer carries away samids (a particular variety of sticks) of a Sage. The Sage cries for help since without them he cannot perform his daily karmas. Pandavas decide to help him and run deep into the jungle in search of the deer.

Overcome by thirst from the long chase, they look for drinking water and Nakula finds a lake. When he is about to drink the water he hears a Yaksha's voice asking him not to drink the water until he answers his questions. Without bothering, Nakula continues to drink and falls dead. Other brothers Sahadeva, Arjuna and Bhima follow Nakula and also die. Yudhishtra instead starts answering the questions of the Yaksha. His answers satisfy the Yaksha, who is actually Lord Yama.

Two sample questions and answers:

Yaksha: What should a man abandon, to become lovable, to grieve less, to become rich and to become happy?

Yudhishtra: Abandoning pride, man becomes lovable; abandoning anger, he grieves not; abandoning desire, he becomes rich; abandoning avarice, he becomes happy.

Yaksha: What is the greatest wonder of the world?

Yudhishtra: The fact that people think that they are permanent in spite of the fact that they see with their own eyes several people dying every day. Could there be a greater wonder than this?

Bhishma's upadesa /Advice

Bhishma is lying on the bed of arrows, on the bank of a river attended upon by sages. The great Pitamaha waits or Uttarayana to come so that he can breathe his last. Directed by Sri Krishna, Pandavas request Bhishma to share his wisdom and give guidance. Bhishma gives many dharmic instructions and shares his thoughts with Pandavas in the presence of Sri Krishna. Here is how Bhishma starts: "Strengthened by contemplation upon you, I seem to have turned into a youth; Krishna, by your grace, I am competent to speak of what promotes welfare. "I first bow to Dharma, I then bow to Krishna, the Creator, I finally bow to Brahmins, before I start speaking of the Etrernal Dharmas". Then he goes on.

A few gems in the invaluable Bhishma Upadesa:

- The king would harm himself if he harasses the subjects in his ignorance by imposing taxes not founded in the texts and motivated by thought of income only.
- The world is struck with death and surrounded by old age. Days and nights speed by: one should be always awake. Do welfare and follow dharma; let not time pass you. Even as your acts are not finished, death drags you.
- An aged man, a relative, a friend, a widowed sister, a teacher, and a learned man - these, if they happen to be poor, must be protected by one according to one's ability.
- The continuous meditation of Lord Narayana, worshipping Him, making offerings to Him and singing His praises are all means of realizing the ultimate truth.

Vishnu Sahasranama

It was during Bhishma Upadesa that the very popular and powerful Vishnu Sahasranama Stotra was revealed by Bhishma Pitamaha, from his death-bed, to the world.

To a question by Yudhishtra, the revered Pitamaha gave the Upadesa of this great stotra to Pandavas in the presence of Sri Krishna.

****

OUR SIGNIFICANT RITUALS - SAMSKARAS

In this chapter we discuss some of the Samskaras or sacraments enshrined in the scriptures to guide us in fulfilling our obligations as a Brahmin, during different stages of our lives and beyond.

Almost all the rites except a few provide for a Homa accompanied by the recitation of Vedic mantras in the presence of elders of the family.

In Hindu Dharma, the birth of a child has a distinct religious side to it, and likewise the transition to other stages.

The Samskaras are forty in number. Some of them are:

- Garbhadana (conception)
- Jatakarma (childbirth)
- Namakarana (naming the child)
- Anna prasana (giving solid food for the first time to the child)
- Upanayana (Sacred thread for the boy)
- Vivaha (Marriage)
- Pumsavana } Prenatal ceremonies
- Seemanthonnayana } Prenatal ceremonies

In the pages that follow

- **Upanayana**
- **Vivaha**
- **Antyeshti or Apara karma**
- **Sraaddha**

are discussed in some detail.

UPANAYANA

Vamana Avatara:
Upanayana Samskara being performed for Vamana

One is born a Brahmin from the benefits of good deeds done in earlier births. This is otherwise known as *purva janma karma.* But birth alone does not confer *Brahmanya* on a person. The Rishis have listed quite a few samskaras or Vedic rituals that one to be performed for himself by his parents or elders, and afterwards to be done personally. Then only one can be rightly be called a Brahmana. There are forty such samskaras, and one of the most important among these is the Upanayana or the sacred thread ceremony.

Objective: The main purpose of the upanayana is to take a boy nearer to his Guru and get him accepted by the Guru. The Guru then enables him to learn and understand the Vedas, and through appreciation of the Vedas attain the Ultimate Truth.

At what age? The best time to perform the upanayana is when the boy is seven years old. It is all right to do this samskara at the age 5 or up to the age of 11 - and so it is best done between 7 and 11 years of age. If the boy crosses 11, the Sastras still permit performance of the upanayana till the boy is 16. It is imperative that the poonal or the sacred thread is adorned by the boy at least before he turns 16, for after this age he is supposed to lose his *Braahmanatva* or the right to Brahminism if he has not had his upanayana.

In this day and age, when almost no samskaras is performed strictly as prescribed, all Brahmin parents are advised to at least do the upanayana of their sons at the right age.

Procedure: We are all aware that the adornment of the Yajnopaveeta or the sacred thread is one of important parts of the Upanayana. It is interesting to see how the yajnopaveeta, the sacred thread, is given shape. The basic material for the yajnopaveeta, also known as poonal in Tamil, is cotton thread woven by persons who are qualified to preach Vedas. Married women including widows are also qualified to do this job. A Brahmin then takes the woven material, sits in a clean place, and spins the thread around his fingers in such a way that each loop is 4". He makes 96 such loops, folds the total length 3 times and presses the shortened length till it achieves the desired stiffness. Next he makes this into three circular loops. The edges are knotted twice to make the final product - a circular thread with two knots. While doing so a particular mantra is chanted silently by the person who ties the knot, known as *brahma-mudichchu*. The poonal is worn across the body, from the left shoulder to the right hip. It should not go below the navel: and if it does (this can happen to shorter persons), the extra length should be folded and knotted again, to reduce the length.

The number: A Brahmachari wears one and a Grahasta two. One important and interesting point to note is that a grahasta should never be without a *tritiya vastram* or a third garment over the top of his body in addition to the regular veshti and uttariya. It may happen that he finds himself without a *tritiya vastra* at times, and so some grahastas wear a third poonal, just so that their *niyamas* are not disturbed. This is an extra role played by the poonal.

Rules for adornment of the Yajnopaveeta:

- If the poonal tears or becomes useless, as it happens sometimes, it should be replaced at once, and the new one should be worn with the chanting of the proper sankalpa and mantras.
- Tying keys, pins or dollar coins etc. to the yajnopaveeta is strictly prohibited.
- After upanayana, any karma done without the poonal in place will not get the desired result.

- **Performance manual:** The upanayana should be performed in Uttarayana and in the right lagna and muhurta. Upanayana has now become a major social function in most Brahmin households; and so feasting, inviting guests and video-filming of the event etc. have become inescapable aspects of the function. But at no time should this take precedence over the Vedic rites involved.

Upanayana is essentially a Vedic ritual and not a social function. Strictly there is no room for partying or a social gathering.

The do's and don'ts in the conduct of Upanayana

- An appropriate number of Ritviks (Vedic Pandits) should be invited for performing the japa. This number will depend upon the affordability of the family conducting the Upanayana.

- The materials obtained for the different rites should be of good quality.

- Naandi should be performed thoroughly as prescribed, and not perfunctorily. If possible, *Anna Sraaddha naandi* – that is naandi with homam – is recommended.

- If any prayaschitta is due, it should be done.

- After upanayana the boy is expected to perform samida dana twice a day, till he gets married. For at least four days following the upanayana day, samida dana has to be done. This requires careful planning, well in advance. And the samida dana should be done with devotion.

- The Ritviks and other Vedic scholars called to perform the upanayana should be offered adequate sambhavana (remuneration) and there should be no scrounging in this regard.

Rites involved in the Upanayana: A number of practices have been prescribed as part of the proper conduct of an Upanayana. All these items listed here have to be done along with Veda mantras and hence the father of the boy should perform these with utmost attention and involvement. The following are most important of these rituals.

1. Udakashanti japa
2. Ankurarpana
3. Pratisara bandha
4. Naandi sraaddha
5. Punnyahavachana
6. Yajnopaveeta dharana
7. Kumara bhojana
8. Chaula
9. Adornment of the Brahmacharya emblems
10. Asmaarohana
11. Maunji bandhana
12. Hastagrahana
13. Pradhana Upanayana homa
14. Brahmopadesa (Gayatri mantra)
15. Samida dana
16. Bhikshacharana
17. Pranava-sraddha-medha puja
18. Harati
19. Madhyahnika
20. Brahma Yajna

Of the portions cited , Udakashanti Japa, Ankurarpana, Pratisara Bandhana, Naandi Sraaddha, Yajnopaveeta dharana, Pradhana Homa and Brahmopadesa are very important.

Except a few items like Kumara bhojana, all the rituals above require chanting of Veda mantras and specific prayogas in line with the performer's sutras. It is worth emphasizing that the whole process should be executed with great care, sincerity and faith.

As far as possible, one should try to extend upanayana invitation only to relatives and friends of the community. Upanayana is not a social function for which everyone can be invited. It is a purely *sastrokta karma* and the sanctity is vital. If need be, there can be some other programmes like reception in the evening after the Brahmopadesa where all can be invited for a social gathering. Here also care should be taken to see that the boy's Sandhyavandana does not get disturbed.

Every Brahmin boy for whom upanayana is done at the right age will be equipped with *Brahma tejas* and can advance to great heights in his personal and religious life.

Postponement

Upanayana should not be postponed for silly reasons. Recently I came across a family who had postponed their third son's upanayana as they had been told that three Brahmacharis should not live at a time in a house. This is incorrect.

Similarly in another peculiar case, the boy's Bahamopadesa was postponed because the position of boy's planets according to his horoscope were not conducive. This is also not acceptable. It is against Dharma Sastras to postpone upanayana on any such grounds.

Sandhyavandana

After performance of his upanayana a person should compulsorily do Sandhyavandana. Dharma sastra is categorical on this point: it clearly says that a Brahmin who does not do Sandhyavandana is impure and unfit for any Vedic karma. This is the pivotal karma.

People who complain of not having time to do the full Sandhyavandana can at least do the key sections – **arghya, pranayama, maarjana, praasana, tarpana and Gayatri japa.** These will take just 15 minutes altogether, and these parts can be easily learnt. If these sections are done consistently, one's interest will develop in doing it the proper way.

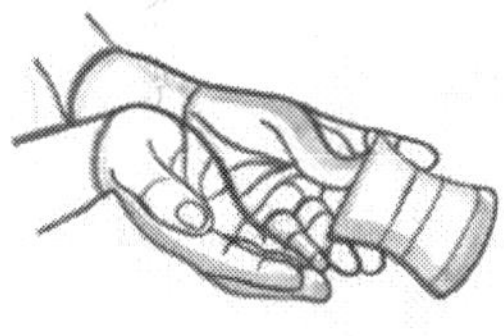

It should be understood that there is no alternative to Sandhyavandana. Going to a temple or attending a bhajan or any other form of devotion does not exempt one from Sandhyavandana. Bhakti marga is truly great, but cannot be in lieu of this key karma. It is worth quoting here the words of Kanchi Maha Swamigal on Sandhyavandana in a lecture in Mudikondan village on 16th December 1939.

"Our ancestors did Sandhyavandana properly and punctually; and there was prosperity and affluence all around. It is now seen that people undertake English education and stop doing Sandhyavandana, which is now done only by persons from Vaidika families and some old families rooted in tradition.

The non-performance of Sandhyavandana and other such key karmas is impacting the health and welfare of mankind at large. Agni worship (fire), the primordial element of Nature, is in danger of disappearing. People ordained to Brahmin karmas should do Sandhyavandana without letup and this will ensure the Agni attains its Poorna jyoti, which will have a salutary effect on the wellbeing of all humankind. The prosperity and affluence of Brahmin families where Sandhyavandana is no longer being done can only be because they come from an ancestry who had religiously observed their karmas, and the momentum of these past karmas is still keeping them going. We feel desolate and shattered when we miss a train or muffle an opportunity, but don't care a hoot if we are missing a Vedic karma of utmost importance – the Sandhyavandana. How thoughtless! The Gayatri mantra in particular is one of the most powerful mantras taught to a Brahmin; and chanting the right number of Gayatri mantras at the prescribed times – or more, if one can – bestows enormous benefits on the person doing the japa".

Look at the different facets of this simple and beautiful ritual:

- It is an upasana
- It is a Yoga
- It is a dhyana
- It is one sure way of viewing one's own soul
- It has great health benefits
- It can lead to prosperity
- It is a prayer for the well-being of the whole world
- It is a nitya karma

Parishechana

The sandhyavandana mantras are somewhat different for various Vedas and there are variations in the mantras between what is said in the morning, afternoon and evening. Enough books are available on these and therefore I will be content with giving the details of Parishechana, which is common to all of us, yet may not available in many books. Parishechana is performed at the start and close of lunch and dinner and everyone after upanayana should do parishechana.

The Process:

1) Keep a Pancha-patra uddhrani (tumbler with a small spoon) of water to your right side while sitting to eat.

2) Touch the banana leaf (or plate) with the right hand ring finger while rice is being served.

3) Take water in the right palm and allowing the water to trickle through the fingers, circle the leaf/plate in a clockwise direction chanting the following mantra while touching the leaf with left hand:

Om Bhurbhuvas-suvaha

4) Sprinkle a little water over the food chanting the following mantra with swara:

Tatsa vitur varenyam bhargo devasya dheemahi,
dhiyo yo naha Prachodayaat.

5) Again encircle the leaf or plate twice with water chanting the following mantras:

Deva Savitaha prasuva / Satyam twartena parishinchaami

At night say:

Deva Savitaha prasuva / Rutamtvaa satyena parishinchaami

6) Aposana: Take a drop of water into your right palm and drink it uttering the following mantra. (It is preferable the person who serves the food serves the water instead of you yourself taking the water):

Amrtopas taranam-asi

7) Prana ahuti (6 times): Then using the three fingers (thumb, middle and ring) take a few morsels of anna (food) and swallow each time chanting each mantra. The rice should not touch the teeth and should be swallowed whole.

Praanaaya swaha

Apaanaaya swaha

Vyaanaaya swaha

Udanaaya swaha

Samanaaya swaha

Brahmmane swaha

8) Now, the person serving food pours a little water on your left palm. Touch your heart with the left palm, touch the leaf with the ring finger of the right hand, and chant this matra.

Brahmmanima Atma Amrutatvaaya

and proceed to eat.

9) Uttaraposana: After you have finished eating, take a little water into your right palm and drink it chanting the following mantra:

Amrutaa pidhaanam-asi

This concludes parishechana (the ritualistic process of eating food).

Summary

It is no exaggeration to say that Upanayana is a fundamental samskara among all the forty Vedic karmas prescribed. Only after a person adorns the poonal he is qualified to do the other karmas. To ignore or treat this basic karma is therefore inexcusable.

A person who has a son and can conduct his Brahmopadesa is indeed blessed. May God give all such parents the right mindset and proper orientation to perform upanayana of their children in the right manner and at the right age!

****

VIVAHA (MARRIAGE)

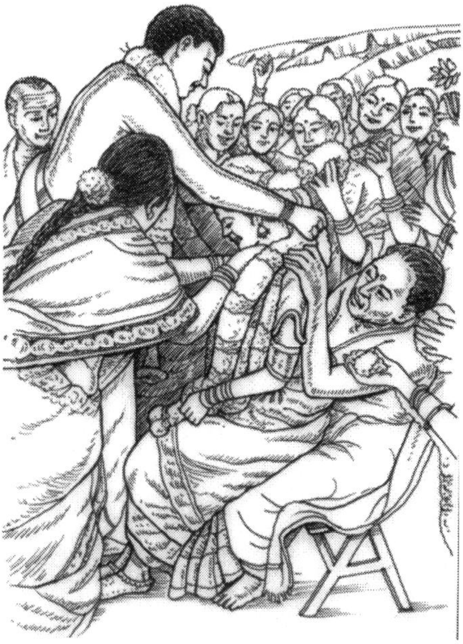

Mangalya Dharana Muhurta

Another important samskara out of the forty samskaras prescribed for Brahmins is Vivaha or marriage. This has to be treated as a Godly ritual and performed with devotion and as per procedure. The key to the processes involved in Vivaha is observance of the Vedic practices specified, in line with the advice of the Sutrakars and giving pre-eminence to the Veda mantras and prayogas.

Of late the laukika or social element of a marriage – reception, music programme etc. – have become integral to a marriage. These are certainly unavoidable and they do give pleasure. But these cannot take precedence over the Vedic rituals, and should be included in the marriage subject to the time and facilities required for the ritualistic parts of the marriage.

Marriages would span four days and more in the olden days, but have now been reduced to two days or a day and a half. But the rites listed for the proper conduct of a Vivaha can be completed in two days or less, and so this is no hindrance.

A marriage has to be seen in the context of the four *ashrams* of a Brahmin's life:

- Brahmacharya
- Grahasta
- Vaanaprasta
- Sanyasa

The Grahasta ashram is an important one among these four, and comes after marriage.

The present generation has almost come to regard marriage as a major social milestone in a man's life - and just that. Most people deem it important that the function should be a grand gala one, celebrated with much pomp and splendour. The entire neighbourhood should be awed by the programmes included: so what if these involve practices alien to our culture?

That the vivaha is in fact a key karma and a Vedic ritual has been totally forgotten.

The proper ritualistic performance of a marriage requires exactitude in many actions, starting with dress as per the dress code. Plaited hair and *madisaar pudavai* (nine-yard sari) are mandatory for married ladies associated with the bride and the bridegroom - and the *pancha kachcham* is similarly a must for men. But even this simple religious practice is not being followed in many marriages these days.

One is acutely conscious of the ravages of time and the need to modify our stance in line with the century in which we are living. But that does not mean we eschew Vedic aspects of a marriage. It is time we sought out our roots and went back in time to some glorious practices ordained for Brahmins - of which vivaha is paramount.

What does marriage bestow on a Brahmin? It is the only recognized permit for other karmas that a grahasta is scheduled to perform, including earning for the family and looking after the family and relatives, dana & dharma, procreation, participating in homas and yagas and pitru karmas.

These and other karmas can only be done by the person with his wife actively involved. Brahmins at other ashrams do not have the right to perform these karmas except pitru karma.

The role of the wife

Observance of *grahasta dharma* calls for the right mindset and a good wife. The lady of the house plays an all-important role in ensuring that the family follows the dharmic path. Her inherent belief in religious rites, sanctity, puja, devotion in other forms, and pitru karma is of great importance to direct her man effectively along the religious path.

The Vivaha mantra, uttered by the bridegroom holding the bride's hand, preparatory to becoming man and wife, is worth calling to our mind here. What does he say? *"The two of us are coming together today, to walk the path of dharma as ordained, perform all our pitru karmas, procreate and in every way consciously do our religious duties."* It is no less than a commitment.

Likewise the bride's father chants as a part of his sankalpa in the kanyadana (giving away the bride): *"I am performing the greatest of danas, the kanyadana, for the satisfaction of my ancestors, in my quest for Brahmaloka, and for the pleasure of Lord Vishnu and the spread of happiness all around".*

The wife is man's support in dana-dharma and all religious duties. She is fundamental to the man's quest for *moksha*. Even at a social level, a married man is more credible and gets a holistic outlook to life and its pleasures.

Events forming part of a Vivaha

Before we begin, one thought: Why not include in the wedding invitation a Sanskrit version, apart from the mother tongue and English? This is not for communication but to emphasise the sanctity of marriage as a Vedic rite and not merely a social function.

The following are some crucial events in the proper conduct of a marriage.

1. Sri Vigneswara puja
2. Sumangali Prarthana

3. Samaradhana
4. Yatra dana
5. Pandhakkaal muhurta
6. Ashta vrata for the boy
7. Jaata karma or Namakarana (naming)
8. Naandi sraaddha (Abhyudaya)
9. Raksha bandhan (kaappu)
10. Sprinkling of paalika
11. Kasi yatra
12. Exchange of garlands
13. Oonjal (the swing)
14. Anujna (Sankalpa for Kanyadana)
15. Kanyadana
16. Placing the nugaththadi (a small plough is placed on the head of the bride by the groom.)
17. Giving the koorai pudavai (the bridal sari) to the bride
18. Mangalya dharana
19. Adorning with the metti (the toe-ring)
20. Tying munjippul (a belt made of darbhai is tied around the bride's waist)
21. Panigrahana
22. Saptapadi
23. Pradhana homa
24. Treading the ammi
25. Laaja homa
26. Untying munjippul
27. Graha pravesa
28. Looking at Dhruva & Arundhati (the stars)
29. Commencing Aupasana, Agneya Stalipaka
30. Gandharva puja
31. Sesha homa
32. Vivaha-anga naandi

The significance of Vivaha rituals

In essence the bride identifies herself completely with the groom through the course of the Vivaha rituals. She is exhorted to follow her spouse in treading the part of righteousness. She is called upon to stand by him through thick and thin lending him full support to face the vicissitudes in life.

We will describe briefly some of the events listed above.

Nischayatartha (engagement)

It is a common practice nowadays to have an elaborate engagement ceremony, where relatives are invited and the engagement is announced. The bride's father promises to give his daughter to the prospective groom. This betrothal is a reconfirmation on the evening of the day before the actual wedding.

Japas

The rituals of the wedding day start with both parties separately performing prayers to purify and prepare themselves for all the Vedic rites. Invitees are received, rose water sprinkled on them, and sandal paste, sugar and flowers offered at the entrance.

This process serves to clear the air of any negative vibrations. Nadaswaram is also played.

Kasi Yatra

Kasi yatra denotes the migration of the boy from Brahmacharya to Grahasta ashram. The boy symbolically walks out of the gate to go to Kasi (Benares) to enhance his knowledge and is called back by the bride's father, who requests him to marry his daughter and start life in his new ashram.

Pancha Kachcham and Madisar

One important symbolism at marriage and after is the attire to be worn by the couple. The bridegroom for the first time is initiated into wearing his dhoti in a manner called pancha kachcham.

He puts this on after his morning prayers and before he starts on Kasi Yatra. Similarly the bride will wear the nine yard sari given away by the bridegroom's side after exchange of garlands.

In our tradition, after the initiation of wearing madisar and pancha kachcham during the marriage, the couple are expected to wear this attire all through their lives.

The attire signals to the world their 'married' status. While it is understandable that men and women today are unable to wear such attire every day, it is desirable that they wear this on important festive and karma days.

Wearing of pancha kachcham and madisaar is quite simple and far more convenient than many people believe.

I have highlighted below the ease with which pancha kachcham can be worn.

The ideal size of the Veshti for wearing Pancha Kachcham could be either:

9 x 5 yards

or

10 x 6 yards

Pancha kachcham in *visuals*

First act:
Roll the poonal (yajnopaveeta) in the right ear as shown in the picture.

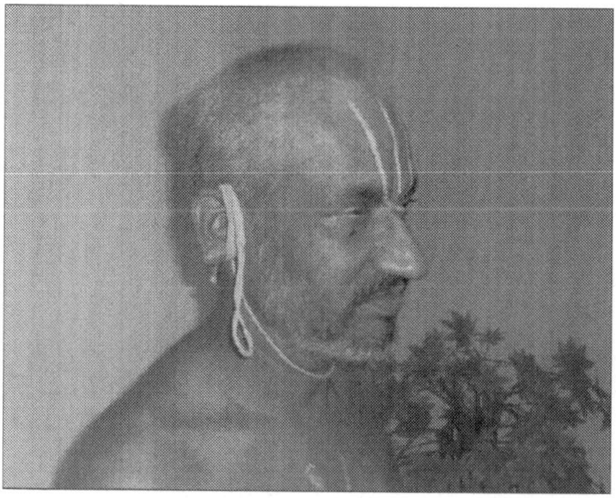

Second act:
Tie the small Veshti (Uttariya) round the head

Now start wearing the Kachcham step by step.

Step 1: *Open the big Veshti completely (9 or 10 yards). Hold it putting it behind you by left hand at one end and at 6th feet by right hand. Measure exactly 3 feet from that left end.*

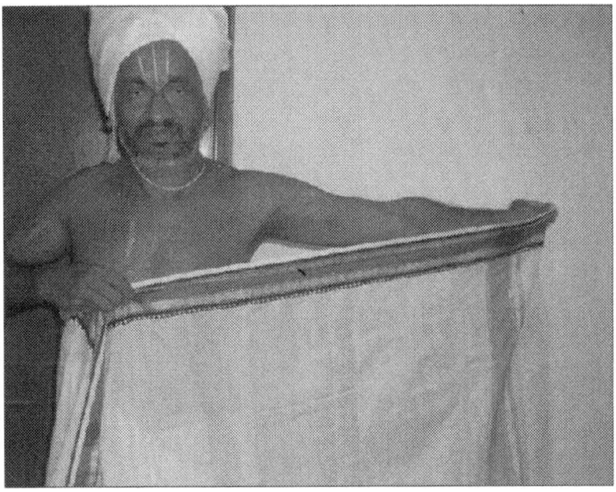

Step 2:
Wrap it around you once (as shown) keeping the wrap a little tight at the stomach.

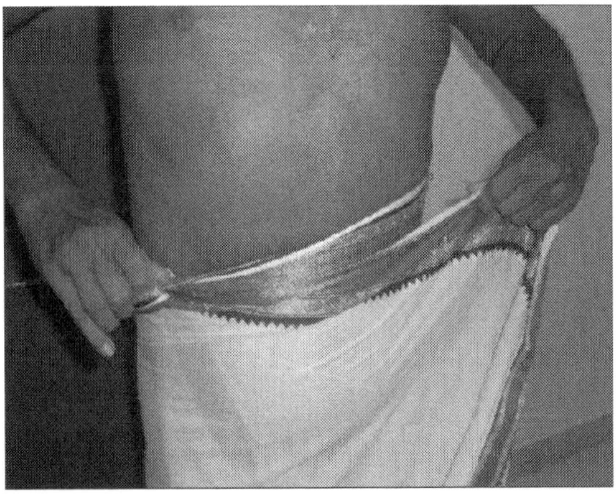

Step 3:
Fold the Veshti a few times (rolling down) so that it is held firmly at your hip. See the pictures.

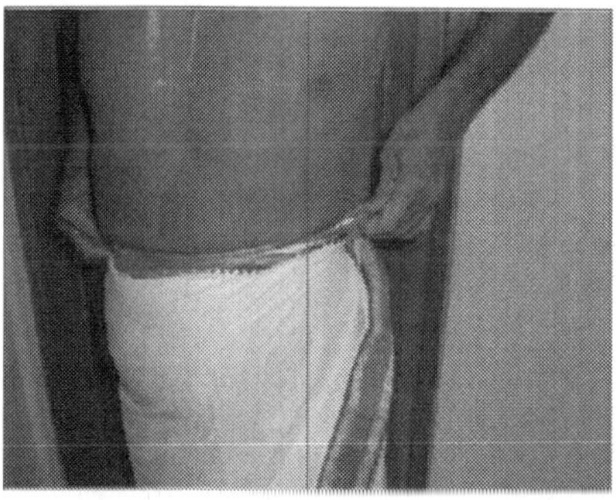

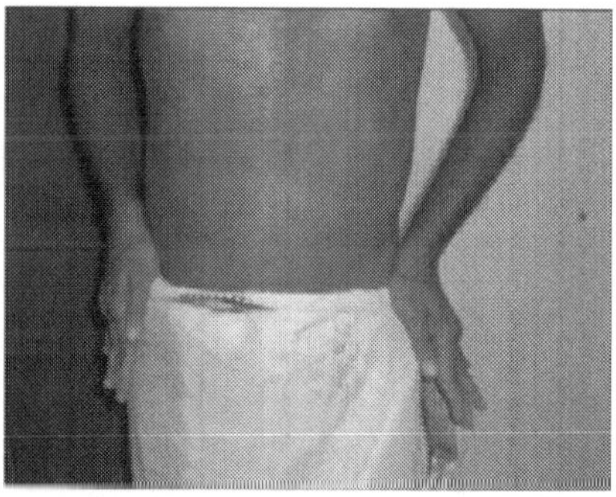

Step 4:
Take the end that is on tip (typically should be the one to your left) start from the end, slowly make folds of about 2 inches left.

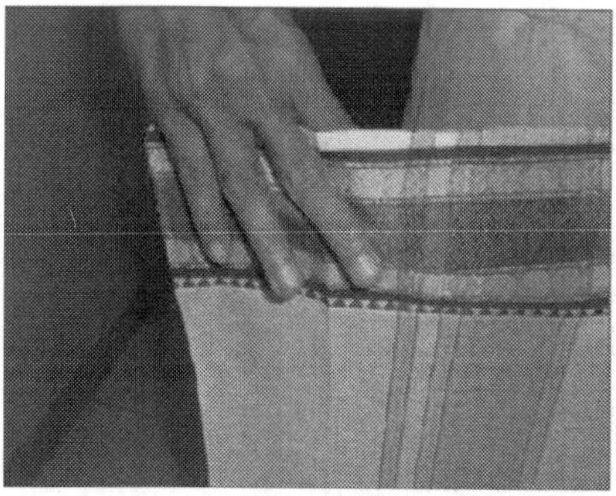

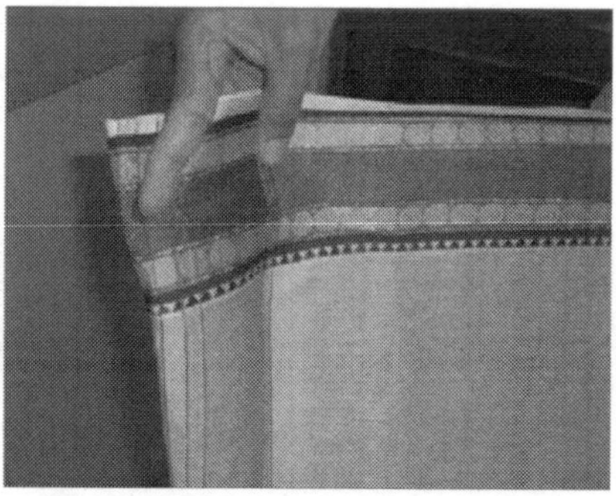

Step 5:
Insert the folds into the wrap just at your Nabhi.

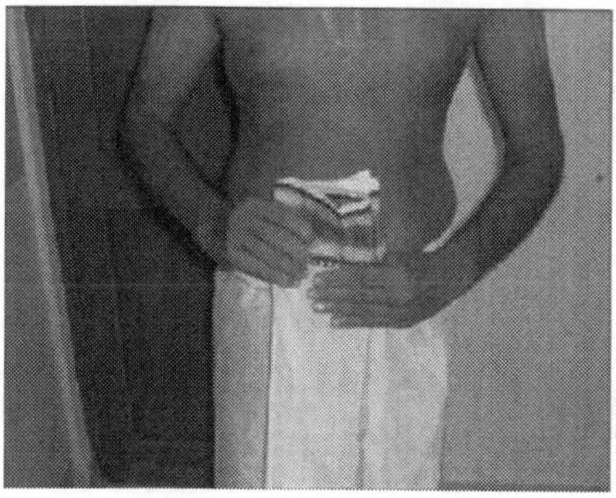

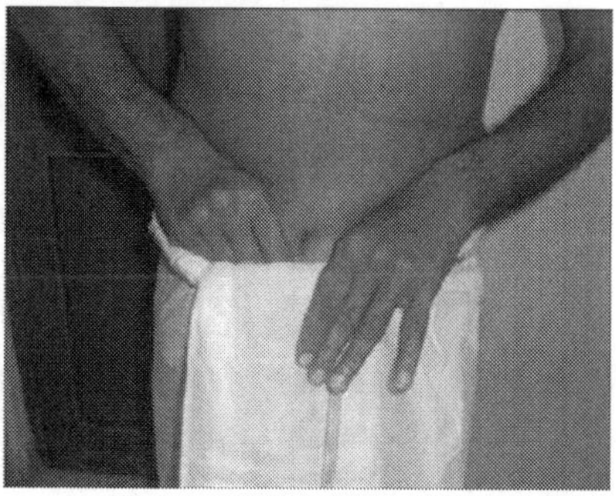

Step 6:
Take other free end of the Veshti, starting breadthwise, make similar folds.

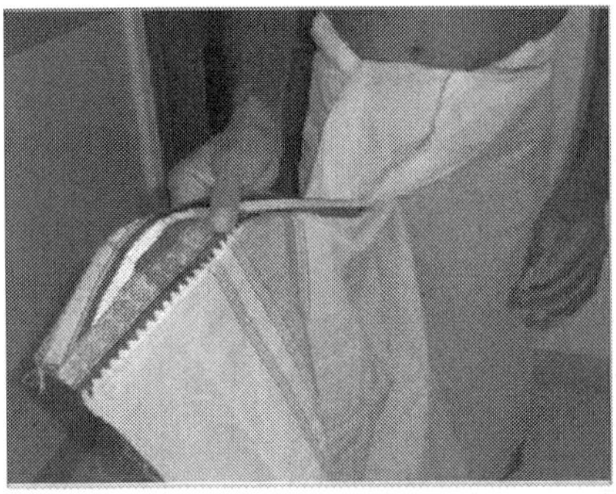

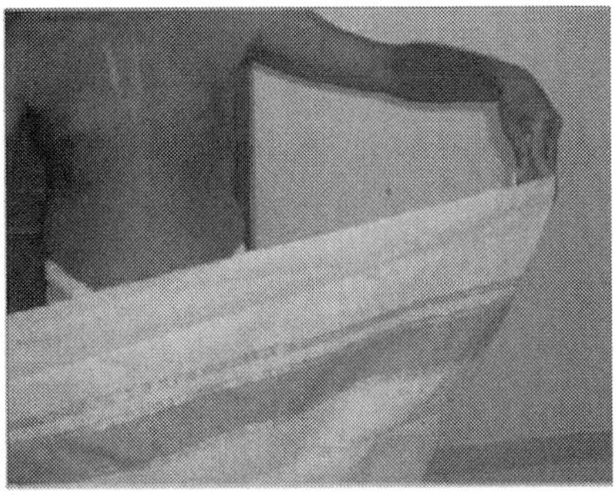

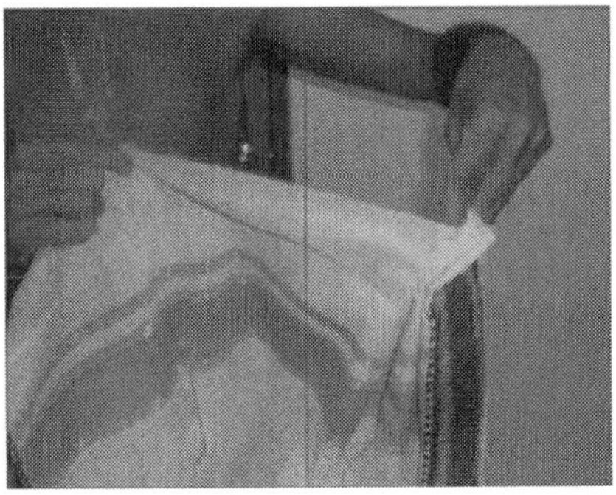

Step 7:
Ensure that the folds are not twisted.

Step 8:

Insert the folded portion at a suitable point in front (as shown) and straighten fold by fold in a straight portion by deeply pressing at the fold edge. Do it repeatedly till it gets straightened and looks neat.

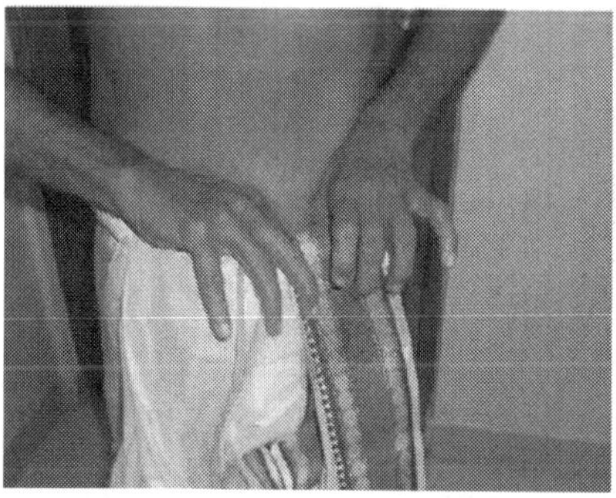

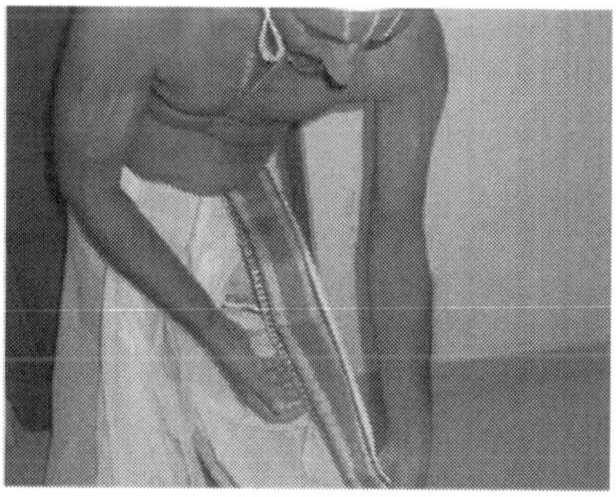

Step 9:

Run this between your legs and bring it up behind you (as shown). Here care should be taken that legs should not be lifted. One should not lift the legs from the ground.

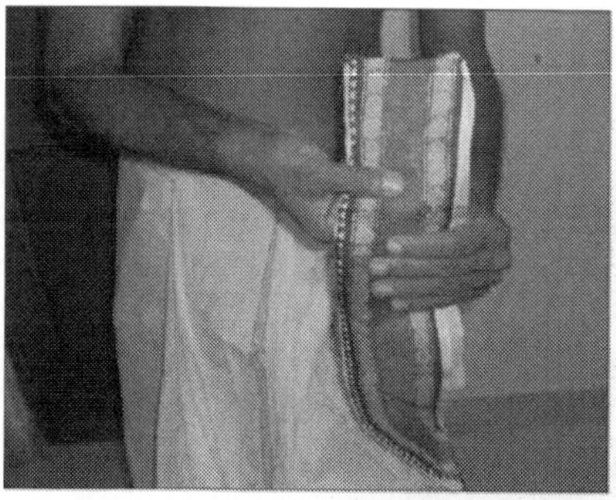

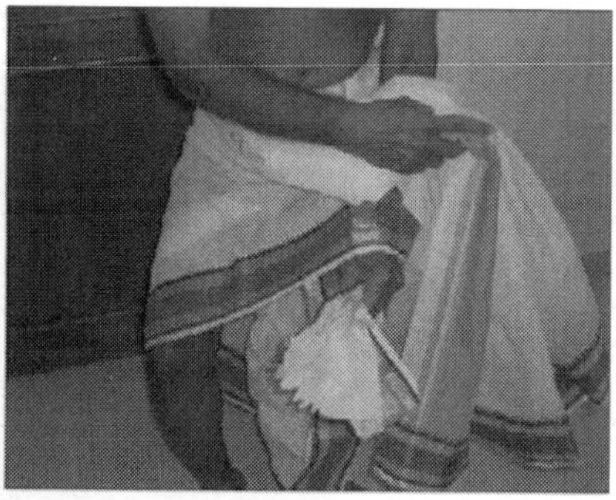

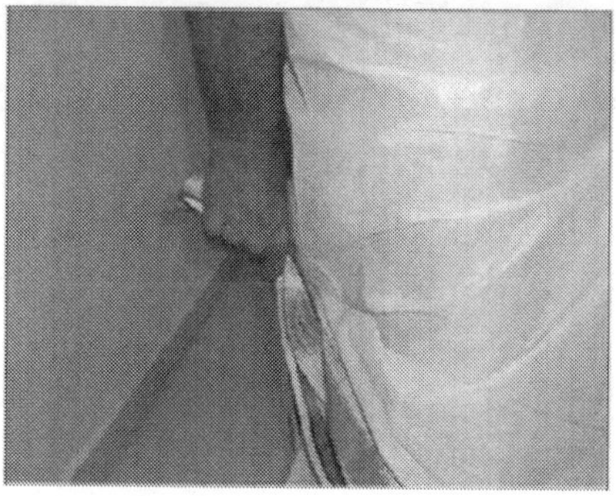

Step 10:

Insert the new set of folds behind your back (as shown)

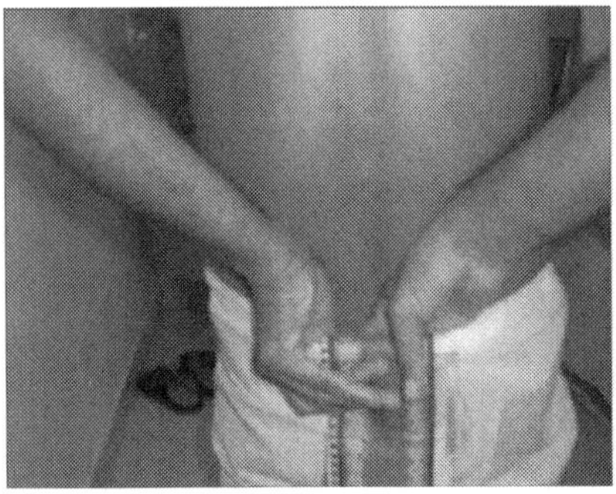

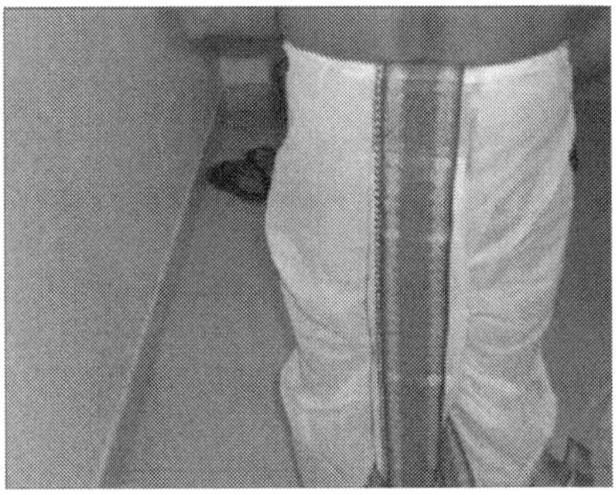

Step 11:

Take the breadth portion of the top fold and starting from the end (so that the bordering colour is visible) make similar folds (as shown)

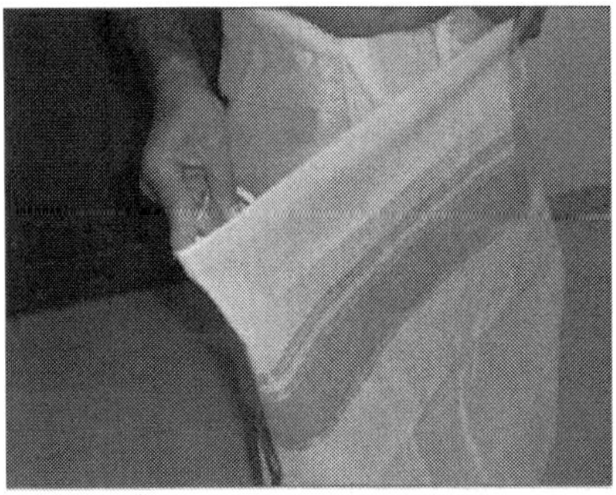

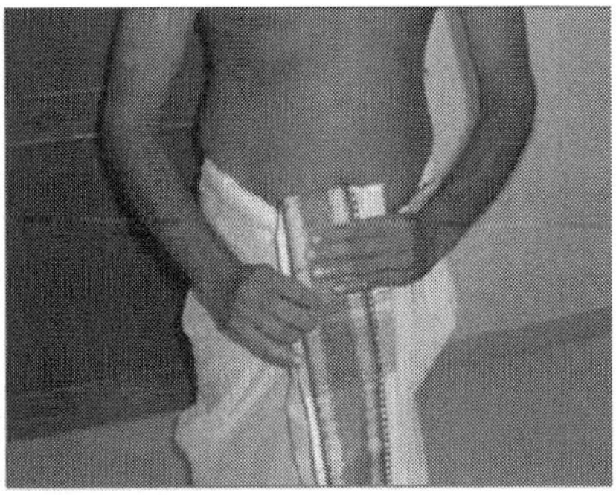

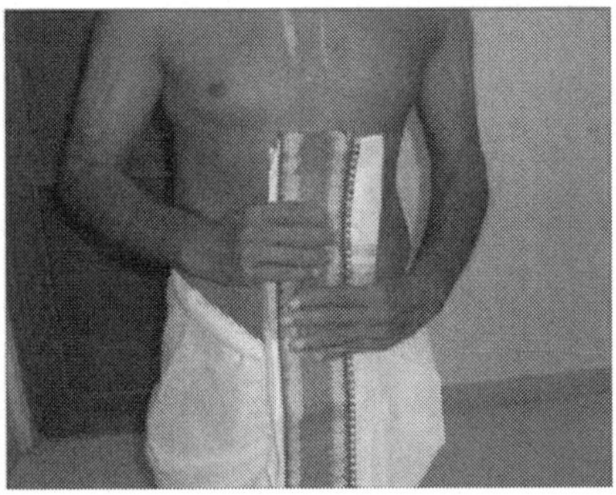

Step 12:
Insert this set of folds (second set) on the top of the previous one in front, just below the Nabhi.

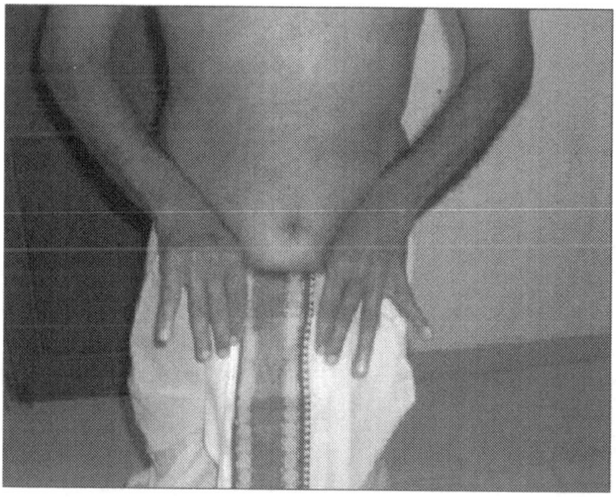

Step 13:
Straighten it fold by fold to make the frontage as shown in the picture.

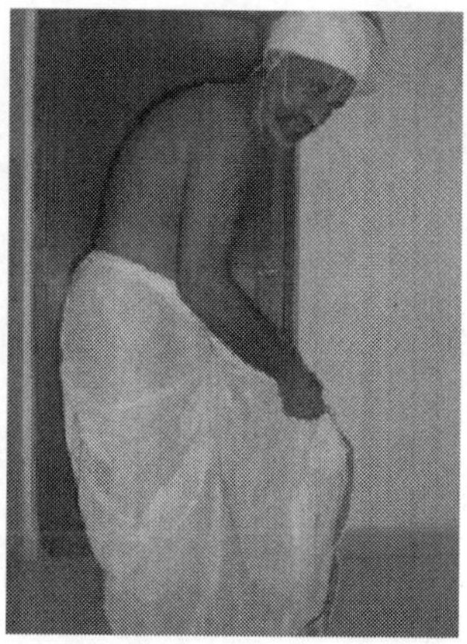

Step 14:
Now bring back the Poonal to its original position and take the small veshti from the head and tie it around the hip as shown (Care should be taken that the Uttariya is not be tied around the main Veshti as belt. It should be tied around the hip above the main Veshti as shown).

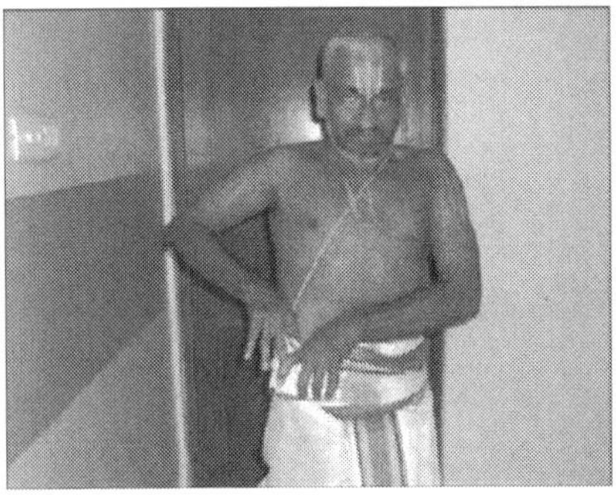

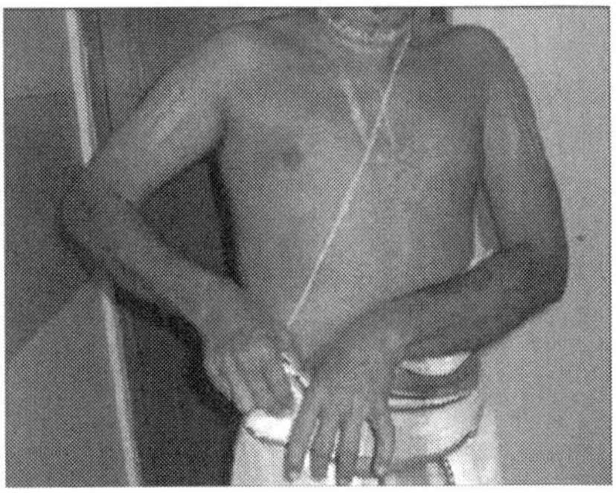

The pancha kachcham should look as shown in the picture.

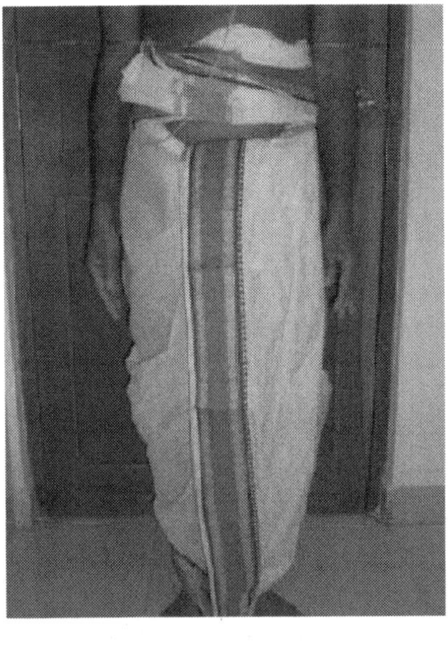

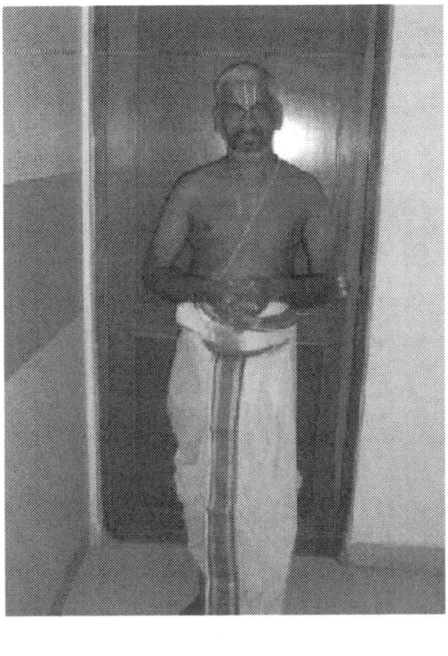

Exchange of garlands

The exchange of garlands denotes the coming together of two individuals and their families. A spirit of joy and vivacity marks this procedure, signifying the strengthening ties between the families.

Oonjal – the swing

After the exchange of garlands the bride and the groom sit side by side on a swing and ladies go around them with lighted lamps and throw coloured rice balls around them, to the accompaniment of devotional singing. The ritual marks the first time the girl and the boy are together. **The bride sits to the left of the groom** (generally it is the other way round).

Kanya dana – giving away the bride

The prospective father-in-law seats the bridegroom facing east and washes his feet personifying him as Mahavishnu. Then in *vadhu sameekshana* the groom and the bride look at each other formally for the first time. He recites dosha nivarana mantra to the Gods Varuna, Brihaspati, Indra and Surya and wipes the eyebrows of the bride with a blade of darbha grass. He then chants *rodana prayaschitta* mantra to ward off the effects of the cry of parents on account of the separation of their daughter.

Vadhu parishuddhi – Sanctification of the bride

During this ritual a small yoke is kept on the bride's head and a piece of gold placed upon it. Water is poured through the hole of the yoke chanting Veda mantras. The yoke and gold signify auspiciousness. The blessings of the Gods are invoked in the water.

Five Veda mantras are recited to sanctify the bride in preparation for the subsequent stages of the wedding. This aspect of the wedding is known as the mangala snana (vadhu snana).

Surya, Varuna and other Gods are invoked. These rites for the girl are similar to the sacred thread ceremony (upanayana for the boy). This is followed by vastra dana when the bridegroom gives the wedding dress (koorai pudavai) to the bride invoking Lord Indra through a mantra. The bride for the first time initiated into wearing this sari in a manner called madisar.

Mangalya dharana

At the auspicious moment already fixed, the bride is seated on her father's lap and the bridegroom takes the sacred thread (mangalya or thali) and fastens the first knot around the neck of the bride. His sister fastens two more knots.

This is done to the accompaniment of a beautiful sloka which means:

"This is a sacred thread. This is essential for my long life. I tie this around your neck, O maiden! May you live happily for a hundred years (with me)!"

Yoktra dharana – tying the darbha girdle:

This is the next step, done with the following mantra:

"This bride seeks benevolence, health, progeny and non-widowhood. She is now ready to follow all Vedic rituals with me. For this purpose I tie this girdle around her waist."

The bride is next led near the Agni, sacred fire, for conducting the rest of the wedding ceremony. The bride and the groom sit on a new mat in front of the Agni. The groom recites three mantras which invoke Soma, Gandharva and Agni to give strength, beauty and youth to the bride.

Panigrahana – holding the bride's hand

After mangalya dharana the groom clasps the right palm of the bride with his right palm covering all the five fingers and recites mantras in praise of Bhaga, Aryama, Savita, Indra, Agni, Surya, Vayu and Saraswati. The bride's fingers are said to represent her heart. The ritual symbolizes the bride surrendering her heart to the groom and the beginning of a new relationship. The meaning of the mantras is: *"I hold your hand with the prayer that you will give birth to noble children and live with me until you attain old age. The Gods Bhaga, Aryama, Surya and Indra have given you to me to help me perform the duties of a householder as prescribed by Dharma."*

Saptapadi – The seven steps

During this ritual, the groom walks with the bride to the right of the sacred fire holding his wife's right hand in his right hand. He helps her take seven steps around the fire. At the beginning of each step, he recites Veda mantras to invoke the blessings of Mahavishnu to guard his wife and bless her.

After the seventh step is taken the groom looks at her and chants the 'prasuka' mantra: *"Oh bride! You have walked seven steps with me; you are now my companion. Neither of us will forgo this companionship. We will decide our obligations and carry them out with mutual love and goodwill. We shall strive for a common vision. You are the earth and I am the sky. I am the semen; you are its bearer. I am the mind and you are speech. You are Rig mantra and I Sama mantra. May you be supportive of my pursuits".* With these two rituals the bride and the groom attain the status of husband and wife.

Pradhana homa

After *Saptapadi*, they take their seats on the western side of the Agni, sacred fire, and conduct pradhana homa, when the bridegroom seeks the blessings of Lord Indra and other deities. During the conduct of this homa, the bride must place her right hand lightly on her husband's body to get the full benefit of participation.

***Asmarohana* or treading the millstone (ammi)**

Here the husband holds the right toe of his wife, lifts her leg gently and places it on a flat granite grinding stone (ammi in Tamil). The ammi is placed to right of the Agni.

Laaja Homa

This is a homa with parched rice (pori in Tamil). Here the bride cups her hands and her brother fills the cupped hand with the puffed rice. The husband adds a drop of ghee to the rice and recites five mantras. At the end of each mantra, the puffed rice is offered to the sacred fire as havis (offering). After each offering, they go round the Agni thrice and the bride steps on the ammi. The three mantras chanted during pradakshina (circumambulation) and the mantra chanted while the bride steps on the stone are repeated after each offering. After the Laaja homa and two more mantras, the groom removes the darbha girdle of the bride. With this, all the Vedic ceremonies come to an end.

Nalangu

Nalangu is celebrated in the evening hours after the completion of the marriage rituals. This is basically performed to bring the two families together with a lot of fun and frolic, and to ease the tension of all the rituals. The groom is decorated by the bride and vice versa. In this event all relatives participate.

Grahapravesa and Pravesa homa

At the end of all the rituals, the couple leaves for the groom's house carrying the Aupasana Agni (sacrificial fire). This Agni is supposed to be maintained till the last ritual in one's life. Many mantras are chanted for the safe travel etc. On reaching home, the groom chants prayers to thank all the Devatas for the safe conduct of the marriage. The girl is asked to enter the house with her right foot forward. Pravesa homa is then performed for progeny, health, wealth, longevity and togetherness of the new couple. In the evening, the husband shows his wife the Pole star (Druva darshana) to infuse steadiness in her mind. He later shows her the Arundhati star to inspire her to lead a virtuous life like Arundhati.

Garbhadana: At the end of all the rituals, the husband touches the heart of his wife and propitiates all gods and goddesses for a mutually affectionate life. With a few Veda mantras addressed to Prajapati and Siva, the vivaha becomes complete.

Kanchi Paramacharya on Vivaha

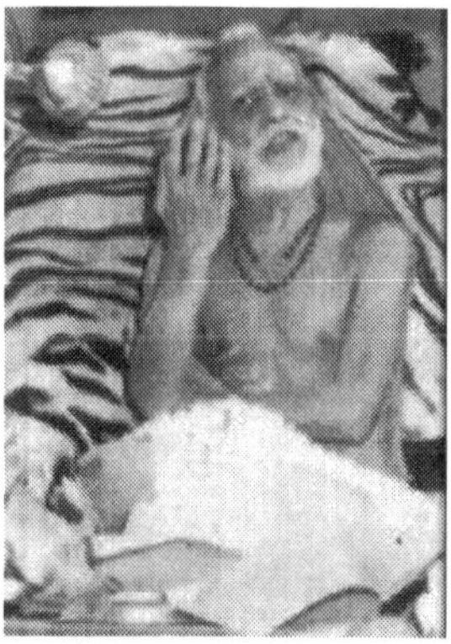

In conclusion, the divine words of Sri Sri Mahaperiyaval of Kanchi on this subject are worth quoting (Courtesy "Hindu Dharma", a book published by Bharatiya Vidya Bhavan) "The Vedas are learned during the years of student-bachelorhood. Then the theory taught has to be put into practice; in other words the rites prescribed in the Vedas must be performed. For this purpose a man has to take a helpmate after he has completed his brahmacharyasrama. This helpmate is a "property" that can never be separated from him. She is not meant not only to be a cook for him, not only one to give sensual gratification. She is called "dharma-patni" and also "yajna-patni". She has to be with her husband in the pursuit of dharma and has also to be a source of encouragement in it. As a dharma patni, she has to be by his side during the performance of sacrifices; she must also play a supportive role in all those rituals that have the purpose of making the divine powers favourable to mankind.

It must be noted that a wife creates well-being for the world even as she does the work of cooking or is a source of sensual gratification for her husband. I will tell you how. It is not that she cooks for the husband alone. She has to provide food every day to the guests, to the sick and to the birds and beasts and other creatures. This is how she serves the purpose of "atithyam" and "vaisvadevam". The children born to here are not to be taken as the product of pleasure she affords her husband. She gives birth to them to perpetuate the Vedic dharma. Yes, even the raising of sons is intended for the dharmic life of the future. No other religion has before it such a goal for the marriage samskara.

In our religion the man-wife relationship is not concerned with the mundane alone. It serves the Atman as well as the good of mankind. In other religions too marriages are conducted, say, in a church with God as witness. But ideal of marriage is not as lofty as ours. The purpose of marriage in our religion is to purify the husband further and to make the wife his devoted and self-effacing companion. There is no such high purpose in the marriage of other religion. In other countries the man-woman relationship is akin to a family or social contract. Here it is an Atman connection. But this very connection is a means of disconnection also - of freeing the Atman, the self, from the bondage of worldly existence. There is no room for divorce in it. Even to think of it is sinful.

[To sum up and further explain] The three objectives of Vivaha samskara: The first is to unite a man with a helpmate after he has completed the study of Vedas. This helpmate is expected not only to run his household but assist him in the practice of the Vedic dharma. The second is to bring forth, into this world, children of noble outlook and character who are to be heirs to the great Vedic tradition, citizens of the future who will be the source of happiness in this world. The third is to create a means for women to be freed from worldly existence. A man who is not yet fully mature inwardly is assisted in his karma by his wife.

By doing so, by being totally devoted to her husband, she achieves maturity to a degree greater than he does. The fourth objective is sensual gratification and it is distinctly subordinate to the first three. But we have forgotten the first three important objectives. All that remains is the fourth, the enjoyment of carnal pleasure. If people take my advice in respect of the noble ideals of marriage as taught in the sastras a way will open out to them for their inner advancement. May Chandramaulisvara bless them".

****

APARA KARMA or ANTYESHTI

There is a great deal we need to know about our Dharma and Karmas and about Hindu culture and tradition. We also need to continually clarify our questions and doubts in these subjects. One such subject that is important is *Apara Karma,* also known as *Antyeshti and Charama Samskara* – the religious duties to be performed upon the death of one's near relatives. These duties or rituals are collectively referred to as Apara karma.

What is given here is intended for believers in samskara who want to do their karmas religiously but do not know how to, or know peripherally but seek more clarity. This is not meant for non-believers who do not want to do their karma. This section of the book tries to clarify doubts that come up often, and to answer some FAQs.

I must add here that the subject is truly vast, and this chapter is just a summary. To know more, to get into the intricate details, you can approach your elders or contact me.

Death is inevitable

We all understand one thing: from the moment a person is born he is moving towards death. The mind does not easily accept it when a person close to us is 'no more' – and believes that he has in fact attained *paraloka*, that jiva (the soul) cannot be destroyed though the sarira (the body) can be.

This is correct. A sinner suffers the effects of his bad deeds by going to hell, and a saintly person realises the results of his good deeds and goes to heaven.

In the after-life a person achieves *saalokhya* when he gets into devaloka; he achieves *sarshtita* when he can get the wealth of devas; and he achieves *saayujya* when he becomes a deva himself.

The necessity for Apara karma

While the deeds of a person when alive have a great deal of impact on his station after death, the apara karmas done for him after his death by his son or the karta have an equally crucial impact. Regardless of how the person conducted his life, if his (or her) *Charama samskara* is not done properly, his 'preta' is not released from his body, because he continues to suffer from the same sensations that prevailed during his life. He will feel the sadness from the shortcomings in his Apara karma, and that is good neither for him nor for his family.

When a grahasta dies, two kinds of death rites are possible.

- Brahma medha samskara
- Paitru medhika samskara

Brahma medha samskara is a specialised variety that is performed when the deceased person himself had done Veda adhyayana and the Karta is also familiar with Veda mantras. Paitru medhika samskara which is discussed here is the general ritual, for all the others.

The essence of Apara karma

Apara karma, which spreads over 12 days, should be done by a dutiful son or the Karta properly, and under suitable guidance of the Purohit and elders. He can repay his debt of gratitude to his parents in no better manner than doing their death rites with sincerity, devotion and above all complete faith. In essence, the objective of funeral rites is to facilitate the migration of the soul of a dead person from the status of *preta* to the abode of the *pitrus.*

Apara karma is done in two phases: the rites during 12 days immediately after death, called Apara Karma; and the performance every month thereafter for 12 months on the same day (tithi), called Maasika. In addition, there are Sodakumba Sraaddhas, four Una masikas to the performed over the year.

Two features of Apara Karma can be called the essence of the ritual.

- The mantras pronounced correctly and in proper order
- Doing danas (gifts)

Mantras: The Purohit who conducts the karma will take care of the mantras, and it is enough if the Karta and his family cooperate with him. His directions should be followed implicitly and the mantras repeated accurately; there should be very little disturbance during the performance; and the timings indicated by him should be maintained.

Danas: Dana is however entirely in the hands of the Karta. The quantity and quality of Dana should be decided by him in consultation with the Purohit. Any short-changing by the Karta in offering danas can affect the benefits of the karma.

People who live in big cities like Chennai understandably cannot afford to do the karma at home, as they live in small flats in crowded localities. They seek public institutions that are built especially for the conduct of such rituals. Some of these also provide free services for underprivileged people.

This is a reprehensible practice: People who can afford to spend should not hesitate to spend what they can for satisfactory performance of apara karma. Scrounging in this matter reflects ingratitude to the pitrus and this may have adverse effects later.

Poor people who wish to do karma properly but are unable to, can approach their Purohit who will certainly help to perform the karma in a way that the Karta can afford. Money is not the yardstick for how well the rites are performed: the essence is to do what you can, but do it effectively and with total involvement.

The observance of karmas in general and apara karma in particular has a lot to do with how and in what circumstances a person is brought up. But disciplined and devoted conduct of this antyeshti has great benefits for many generations of the family.

Likewise, the karma done casually or irregularly can have

unfavourable results.

Vedas & Sutras

The great Sutrakars, Apasthamba, Bodhayana, Asvalayana, Drahyayana and others have, without any self-interest, given us a comprehensive manual called 'Apara Sutra', which contains rules and regulations for the ceremonial rites to be performed after death, for the welfare of the living as well as for the delivery of the departed soul. The deceased person has to cleanse himself of the worldly impurities and travel to pitruloka and be transformed into a pitru. This happens through the process of apara karma. Veda Vyasa Maharshi has, in 'Garuda Purana', elaborated on the importance of apara samskara and *Jeevana Sanchara*.

We are also fortunate to have today with us Purohits in large numbers who can perform apara karma properly and effectively. They are professionals and no sambhavana paid to them can be an excess. It is therefore essential that each one of us understands this samskara and does it to the best of our ability.

Sections of Apara karma

The complete set of apara karmas has been segregated into seven sections for convenience.

1. Karna mantra and Dahana (cremation)

2. Nitya Vidhi

3. Sanchayana

4. Dasaaham (10th day rites)

5. Ekadasehani or Vrushabhodsarjana (on the 11th day)

6. Dwadasehani or Sapindikarana (on the 12th day)

7. Griha yajna or Subhasweekarana (on the 13th day)

These seven steps can be viewed as falling into 3 stages:

1. For the sareera (body)

2. For the preta: the *preta* refers to a transient form that the person who has departed takes, which is distinct from the dead body - these are not the same)

3. For the pitru: after the *preta* has departed the rites to be performed to help the *preta* attain pitru status

We will now see each of the seven steps in some detail:

1. **Karna mantra & Dahana:** The body is the vehicle that brought us to this world. It is our identification and our concrete form when we are alive. It deserves to be given a respectful send-off on death, and this is what is done in this step. The body is cleansed with purifying mantras and offered to Agni in this process, the process of cremation.

   The body is not our creation, and so we have no ownership rights to it. It is created by the *pancha bhootas,* viz., *prithvi, akasa, jala, vayu and agni,* and has to be sacrificed to the same *pancha bhootas.* This is why the Sastras have even presented alternative courses of action in case the body is mutilated in an accident or is untraceable.

Sastras also provide for exceptional cases like when the deceased person wants to donate parts of his body, and have prescribed the *prayaschitta* to be done in such an event.

As far as possible - strictly from the standpoint of proper observance - donating the body or parts of it to medical colleges or hospitals should be avoided, for in such cases the body may not be cremated - and cremation is absolutely essential.

Question: Are Karna mantra and Dahana samskara the same?

Answer : No. They are different: Dahana follows Karna mantra.

Karna mantra is the function to be performed before cremation. Ideally this should be done just before death, even as the life is ebbing away.

Process of Dahana: The Karta has a quick bath without use of soap etc. and sits on the ground with wet clothes. He wears only a single cloth. The Purohit guides the rituals. After the homa and related mantras the body is taken to the cremation ground. The grandson(s) carries a ghee-flame and walks a few steps in front of the body (van). The karta carries Agni in a pot and accompanies the body to the burial ground. After elaborate rituals the body is handed over to the officials at the crematorium and they take care of the actual job of cremation.

A significant change these days is the increasing popularity of electric & gas crematoriums in urban areas in preference to manual burning. Both forms of cremation are acceptable, but strictly from a traditional perspective manual burning is preferable. The rituals and rites to be observed before cremation are of course the same in both formats.

Pashaana sthaapana: As soon as the body is cremated, Pashaana-sthapana (preta avahana) is to be done. This is done by installing three sets of two stones each in the *tadaaka tira* (lake bed) and in the *griha-dwara* (entrance of the house), to the accompaniment of mantras.

2. **Nitya Vidhi:** On completion of cremation the *preta* is rid of the body, but it suffers from a terrible thirst and burning sensation. The *vaasanas* (sensations) have not left the preta yet, although the bodily connection has been severed. Nitya Vidhi provides the answer for quenching the thirst and the burning.

   In this step, as we have seen above, small stones are buried in two different places with mantras. If the rituals take place in a village, one such set of the Pashaana sthaapana is done in the house (griha dwara kunda) and the other one near some water body (tadaaka tira kunda). Tarpanas of two different types like *Tilodaka* and *Vasodaka* are done, apart from *pinda-pradana* etc. all through the ten days from the date of death.

A crucial prerequisite is that the

- Vastra used for the Nitya Vidhi (Vasodaka),
- the brass water-can (pithalai sombu),
- the utensil in which the pindam is cooked,
- the places of performance and
- the Vastra worn by the Karta

should be the same day after day, and should not be changed through the 10 days.

The rice for the *pindam* should be cooked after bath and in the wet by the daughter of the deceased person or any other lady.

As part of Nitya Vidhi, two sraaddhas called *Ekottara Vriddhi* sraaddha and *Nava*-Sraaddha should be performed in hiranya format i.e. Brahmins should be invited and offered rice, pulses and unripe banana (in vegetable form and not fruit) besides dakshina.

3. **Sanchayana:** This step deals with the dissolution of the Asti (ashes), collected from the burial ground, in punya-tirtha (holy water). The Asti is worshipped with milk abhisheka and with Vedic mantras. There is a homa too at the cremation ground, prior to the dissolution.

4. **Dasaaham:** Dasaaha is done on the **10th day,** as the name indicates. The rite starts with the regular Nitya Vidhi, after which the *Jnyatis* (meaning people who are required to observe theettu (quarantine) throughout the ten days) take bath and without their uttariya and without combing their hair go to the lake bed and do the ten days' tarpana in one sitting. The younger *Jnyatis* should have Vapana – shaving of the head – as well

before undertaking the tarpana. The Karta then takes over and does that day's tarpana.

This is the stage in which the preta has to start travelling to *pitruloka*. The 10th day is also the day when the preta is consumed with hunger that needs to be appeased. We do this by offering it *Prabhoota bali*, which consists of large amounts of not very well made food, almost dumped on the preta. The rice is half-cooked, and the vegetables are raw or overdone. There is no salt in the gravy or sugar in the sweets, and though none of the items are missed out, they are far from edible. The preta is so hungry that it devours the food despite its tastelessness, and then probably gets the message: "they do not want me here anymore, which is why they have thrown bad food at me. It is time I departed to pitruloka". Thus, *prabhoota bali* achieves two purposes, of quenching the hunger of the preta and starting it off on its journey to pitruloka.

Pashana utsarjana: After this, the Pashana sthapana at both the *tadaaka tira kunda* and *griha-dwara kunda* are uninstalled and immersed with a prayer to the *preta* that it may go off to its appointed place.

The Karta then has his head shaved (Vapana), takes bath and performs two homas: Shanti homa and Ananda homa. The programme concludes with Punnyahavachana.

Planting of a tree: A very interesting ritual that has been prescribed between the two homas is the planting of a tree by the Karta. This is one of the actions on the 10th day, and gives us heart-warming evidence of how farsighted our ancestors were, how profound our Vedic rituals are. Imagine the lush richness our landscape could have achieved if each of the succeeding generations had observed this simple ritual! Presumably there would have been no necessity for the multibillion dollar ecology industry.

Charama sloka: The same evening, the evening of the 10th day, there is a tradition of chanting of Charama sloka and offering appam and some other sweets to the invited group of people. It is almost like a condolence meeting with a traditional ritual attached. Charama sloka comprises reminiscences of the dead person's adherence to dharmika karmas, details of the time and date of his demise, and the karmas being done for him from the 1st to the 13th day. This ritual is done on the 13th day in some houses.

The chanting of the sloka and the Upanyasa is generally done by the Purohit who conducts the entire apara karma. The congregation is usually of all the near relatives.

5. **Ekadasehani:** With sunrise on the 11th day the *theettu (quarantine* or tainted period) goes off completely. The house has to be washed and cleaned fully, clothes scrubbed neat, and karmas should start on a pure note. Of course, the theettu again comes to the Karta and those who are present there for a limited period, of that day's karma, and goes off with a bath after the ritual is over. Sri Rudra homa and japa are done here. Then follows the puja of Rishabha (the bull) in the form of a rite called Rishabhodsarjana. This is for attainment of punnyaloka, and 3 kinds of homas and a variety of four Danas have been prescribed on the 11th day. For Vaishnavites, there is some variation here. *Adya-masika Ekoddista* is performed.

6. **Dwadasehani (Sapindikarana):** This day has great significance. Doing Sapindikarana on the 12th day the *preta* obtains the form and characteristics of a pitru and joins the other pitrus. Pitrus live in *pitruloka* in three forms: *Vasu, Rudra* and *Aditya*. If Sapindikarana cannot be done on the appointed day (the 12th day) one should look for the next available date and complete it without any further delay.

This is done on the lines of a Sraaddha and is considered equally important. This karma has to be done in the Aupasana Agni by the eldest son.

A number of Danas of various kinds including Godana (donation of a cow) are prescribed. Some of the Danas specified are:

- Godana
- Bhoodana
- Naukadana
- Pancha Dana (five different varities)
- Dasa Dana (ten different varities)
- Dwadasa Sravanaal Dana (Twelve articles)

Dwadasa Sravanaal: Out of these Danas, Dwadasa Sravanaal Dana merits an explanation. Lord Brahma created 12 sons called Dwadasa Sravanaal and directed them to brief Yamadharma Raja (the God of Death) about the good and bad deeds that the *jiva* had done. On this day of Sapindikarana the karta remembers the 12 powerful Sravanaal and offers danas to 12 Brahmins chanting mantras so that the departed soul would be benefited in the assembly of Yamadharma Raja.

People who can afford it can also do danas such as graha-dana, an amount in lieu of Kanyaka dhana or an Upanayana, a Kalpaka Vruksha (Coconut tree) etc. Offering gold and silver as dana are considered effective as well. Sastras speak very high of the danas done on this day. Though the danas are aimed at the departed soul, these are also greatly beneficial to the Karta.

On this day towards the end of the main programme another Sraaddha, known as *Paatheya* sraaddha is performed. After the main programme, after bathing *Sodakumba* sraaddha is to be performed.

7. **Griha Yajna (Subha Sweekaara):**
   This celebration happens on the last (13th) day. Udaka Shanti japa and Navagraha homa are performed specially on this day. (For Vaishnavites, there is a different set of rites here) Auspicious items like flowers, sandalwood, saffron etc. (mangala dravya) are accepted from the Purohit, who offers these to the karta with chanting of mantras. Brahmana bhojana (feast offer to Brahmins) is also a part of this function. In the morning kolam is drawn both in the Puja room and at the gate, front door and doorstep.

Some frequently asked questions (FAQs) on apara karma:

Qn. Are there any do's and don'ts, on enquiring of a person who is bereaved?

Ans. Yes. Some basic rules are still valid, though a lot has changed now. These are:

- We should not "dress for the occasion".
- We should not touch the 'karta', the person who is doing 'karma' for the departed soul.
- Once karma has commenced, it is not advisable to leave the place till the body has been taken out for cremation. Of course, one can leave the place before the karma starts.
- During the first ten days starting with the day of death, it is better for non-jnatis to avoid eating or drinking in the house in which the death has taken place.
- It would be most appropriate to visit the bereaved person on the day of the demise itself, and ask if he needs any help. If you are knowledgeable about the karmas and rituals to be observed, you can advise the karta. But imposing your views on the priests or interfering in their methods should be avoided. You should show sensitivity to the persons involved and their feelings. While on the subject, some visitors advise the karta to do a simplified

version of the karma to keep the effort and the costs down. This practice is condenmable, and apart form confusing the karta who would have done the karma properly, this accumulates as a sin for the adviser. We should encourage the Karta to do it as prescribed, to the extent possible; or just keep quiet.

Qn. Who are the Jnatis?

Jnatis can be divided into two kinds: Sapindas and Samanodakas. Sapindas are 10-day daayaadis, and Samanodas 3-day dayadis.

Ans. What is 'Aasaucha'?

Aasaucha is the Sanskrit word for the Tamil word 'theettu'. This can be roughly translated as an impurity or a taint and arises at the time of death (or birth) that happens in a family to the relatives of the person dying or being born. This impurity is temporary and its period has been determined for different relations. On completion of the period fixed, the taint goes with a bath. If the asocuchi - the person concerned - is not well and cannot take bath, someone else can take bath ten times, on his behalf, touching him each time. With *Punyahavachana* the impurity gets cleared completely.

Qn. What are the observances associated with aasaucha?

Ans.

a. Aasauchis, viz. people affected by the impurity or aasoucha, cannot go to a temple.

b. They cannot make obeisance (namaskara) to or accept obeisance from an unaffected person.

c. If the taint is because of a death in the family, they should bathe daily in the morning, sleep on the floor and avoid cohabitation.

d. If there is an eclipse midway through aasaucha, the theettu does not apply during that period i.e. till the eclipse is over for *jnatis*. The japas, danas and tarpanas to be done can however be done during the eclipse.

e. The aasaucha applies to a person's house and other belongings.

f. People who observe Ekadasi vrata should not observe the vrata if they are asauchis.

g. Aasaucha does not affect brahmacharis.

h. Aasaucha does not affect Sandhyavandana, which has to be performed. But Veda Adhyayana should not be done during aasucha.

i. Aasauchis cannot make or accept dana.

j. Deva puja, sraaddha and tarpana are also to be avoided during aasaucha.

Qn. How does one keep count of the period of asaucha?

Ans. If the birth or death occurs at night before 1:30 a.m. (18¾ nazhigai) it is considered as the same day (even though in common parlance the day ends at midnight). Some Purohits keep count of the time from sunrise and decide the starting day. Both the methods are acceptable – it depends upon the custom of the concerned family.

Qn. There are variations in taint period (Asaucha Sangraha). Can we get a summary of the different type of taints?

Ans. Here is the summary. (There could be some variations)

Ten-day taint:

1. For the death or birth in the family of a person having ten day taint relation, we have to observe ten day taint.
2. If the male child dies after ten days or if a girl child dies before marriage, the parents, brother and step brother have ten day taint.
3. In case of a boy less than seven years old without sacred thread or more than seven years old with the sacred thread, the members of the family have ten day taint.

Three day taint for men

1. Maternal grandfather
2. Maternal grandmother
3. Uncle
4. Uncle's wife
5. Father in law
6. Mother in law
7. Mother's sister
8. Father's sister
9. Nephew with sacred thread
10. Daughter's son with sacred thread
11. Samanodaka with sacred thread
12. Daughter who is married
13. Sister who is married
14. Biological father in case of adopted son
15. Biological mother in case of adopted son
16. Son who has been given in adoption
17. The son belonging to the clan who is above 7 years and before marriage with three generation of clan relation
18. The son of the clan whose first cropping (choula) has been performed before 25 months.

Taint for one and half days for men

1. Father's sister's daughter
2. Mother's brother's son and daughter
3. Mother's sister's son and daughter
4. Sister's daughter
5. Daughter of Father's brother
6. Daughter of son
7. Daughter's daughter
8. Daughter's son
9. Son of sister who is less than seven years and does not have sacred thread.

One day taint for men

1. Brother, sister and daughter of stepmother
2. Daughters of the above.
3. Wife's brother
4. Daughter of father's step brother
5. Stepbrother's daughter.
6. Father's stepsister
7. Daughter or son of father's stepsister
8. Parents of stepmother
9. Daughters of the clan within three generations who are more than 25 months and lesssix years old and unmarried.
10. Biological brother in case of adopted son
11. Clan members of the biological family
12. Father in law and mother in law who do not have any other children
13. Boys above 25 months and below six years old who have not undergone first crop (Choula) belonging to paternal clan.

Three day taint for women

1. Brother whose sacred thread ceremony is over 2. Brother's son whose sacred thread ceremony is over. 3. Sister's son whose sacred thread ceremony is over 4. Mother of the other wives of husband. Three days taint if death occurs to any of these.

One-and-a-half day taint for women

1. Father's brother 2. Mother's sister 3. Mother's brother 4. Father's sister 5. The children of 1 to 4 above. 6. Paternal grandfather 7. Paternal grandmother 8. Maternal grandparents 9. Sister 10. Sister's daughter 11. Brother's son. Death of any of these persons entail theetu for one-and-a-half days.

One day taint for women

1. Son, daughter, brother, and sister of co-wife's mother 2. Their children 3. Father's stepbrother 4. Father's stepsister 5. Children of 3 and 4 above. 6. Co-wife's parents.

Qn. On the death of his father or mother, if a Karta is advised by his close relatives to do it briefly and not fully, what should he do?

Ans: He cannot do much – in fact even his Purohit cannot do anything because he would get a bad name as an 'interested party'. A lot depends upon the his firmness. Without getting into debates and arguments if he can stand his ground and do as he decides (fully and in detail), that would be the best. If he is indecisive and allows decision to be taken by others then it is fate.

A lasting solution to such issues can be only prevention. We read, study, debate and discuss many things every day – why not include this subject also, without regarding it as inauspicious? Such a mature mindset can provide the correct answers.

Qn. If the Purohit of the relevant sutra is not available what do we do?

Ans. If we cannot get a Purohit who knows the relevant sutra, the apara karma can be carried out with another of a different sutra. But on the 12th day (Dwadasehani) the karma is to be done only as per the sutra of the deceased person.

Qn. What are the karmas to be observed from the end of the 13th day till the day of the first Sraaddha (Abdika), one year later?

Ans. It is said that bodily Vaasanas (sensations) do not disappear easily, and could recur in the first few months after death. For this reason, two monthly observances that have been ordained are *Masika* and *Sodakumba.* Masika sraaddha should be performed every month on the *tithi* on which death occurred. Sodakumba is generally done on the preceding day of the monthly masika. *Oona masika* is done four times in this one year in addition to the monthly masika sraaddhas.

The apara karmas conclude at the end of the first year with an elaborate ritual comprising of Sodakumba, Aabdika Sraaddha and Subha sweekara

****

SRAADDHA

Jeevator Vaakya Karanaat
Pratyabdam Bhuri Bhojanaat
Gayayaam Pinda Dananaccha
Thribhihi; Putraisya Putrata

[Obeying parents when they are alive, performing Antyeshti after their demise, performing Gaya Sraaddha at least once and Pratyabdika Sraaddha every year: these three are expected of a son. Such a son only be called a *putra*.]

Some of us do sraaddha (annual ceremony for deceased parents) perfectly and in great detail every year. But most of us do it regularly, in our own way and as we think fit. For a variety of reasons - shortage of time and space, a host of other preoccupations, and mainly the lack of awareness - it is quite possible that we do not observe certain essentials in the performance of the sraaddha. Quite a few of us feel bad about this and would like to do justice to the performance of sraaddha. It is for such people that this chapter is presented.

Paraloka, pitruloka and pitru karma

A fact that we would do well to remember is that our pitrus live in pitruloka. After the body is cremated they take the shape of a *preta* for some time. Depending upon their own deeds and the apara karma done for them they shed this form after a period and take their place as a pitru in the pitruloka. Sraaddha is the ceremony done for the pitrus.

Our ancestors are known to have performed sraaddha with tremendous devotion and with even more care and diligence than the attention given to special pujas and sankalpas. In the case of puja or venduthal (specific commitment), my father Brahmasri Srinivasa Sastrigal used to say, that if one has difficulty in fulfilling it one can postpone it by tying a rupee coin in a yellow cloth and keeping it till one gets the time and the means to do it. But in the case of sraaddha there is no room for such lenience or deviation. Sraaddha cannot be postponed or done differently from the laid down process.

For whose satisfaction is sraaddha done? Through the performance of a sraaddha we reach satisfaction and happiness to a host of Godly persons:

- The pitrus who always bless us
- Visve Devas, a section of devas who accompany pitrus
- Agni Deva, who participates in the Homa
- Devas, who are immensely satisfied wherever bhojana (food) is offered to brahmins
- People who are consigned to hell, and cannot have opportunity for satisfaction other than through *pinda pradana & vikiraanna,* which are offered during a Sraaddha
- Persons aspiring for pitruloka and unable to attain it
- Other pitrus who are unknown to the Karta

Pitrus' *anugraha* (blessing)

We should develop the faith that pitrus are with us, they can be contacted and we can communicate with them. They are an anga (section) of Devas and can bless us like Devas. Pitrus are gentle persons who can only do good, and who in fact want to do as much good as they can for people of their Gotra.

Satisfaction of the pitrus is said to confer many benefits on the Karta - healthy family, procreation, wealth, wisdom and eminence in life and after-life.

Pitrus' *shaapa* (curse)

We must always be conscious of our Dharmika karma, our religious duty. Increasingly we see instances of Purohits being denigrated, Sraaddha being skipped on some lame excuse etc.

Such behaviour amounts to ingratitude and is unpardonable. Cantankerous arguments on the irrelevance of karmas like Sraaddha in this day and age are to be avoided, and in any case people putting forth such ideas are not interested in the explanations.

Such persons may want to remember that their behaviour can invoke pitru *shaapa* or the curse of pitrus. The Sastras say that pitrus may not even utter a curse – they only have to heave a sigh of petulance or unhappiness, and that can have the impact of a curse.

One would do well to note the sage precept: a person of character performs out of love, but a person without character performs only out of fear. Let us develop character and do karmas with love, not out of fear of being cursed.

The Mantras

Sraaddha occupies the pride of place among all karmas. It is important for the Purohit to spell out the mantras clearly, with proper pronunciation and with the right notes (swaras). It is equally important for the karta to try and repeat the mantras as clearly as he can. This is admittedly difficult for a karta who has not been exposed to Sanskrit or to chanting of mantras, but he should at least try to do his best. The effort matters – the result will come over a period of time.

In the last stage of the sraaddha the karta communicates, through the mantras, some prayers of great import and far-reaching significance for his own happiness and the well-being of his family to the pitrus: *"may we never have to beg, may we always have enough with us to give people who seek alms, may we always remain bound to our Vedas and tradition, and may we always have food at home for the atithi who could come".*

Such profound prayers said with the right chant of the mantras can be tremendously beneficial – this is an incontrovertible fact.

The rules of sraaddha

Sraaddha is performed on the same day, known as tithi of the month (as per the Hindu calendar) every year from the second year onwards. The word Sraaddha comes from *Sraddha,* meaning concentration and care. The karta should be in control of himself during the month or the paksha (half-month) in which the sraaddha is scheduled, or at least for 3 days preceding the function. Control implies eating only at home, and not eating outside except at a brother's place or in his maternal uncle's or in-laws' place. Shaving, having an oil-bath and conjugation are to be avoided.

The process of sraaddha

In the rush and tumble of life today, with many activities we have become accustomed to doing – very often merely for the purpose of 'keeping up with the Joneses' – few of us have the time to do sraaddha perfectly in line with the laid down process. But where there is a will, there is definitely a way.

Firstly, it should be noted that the rules are indeed flexible and take into account the fact that not all people are affluent and can afford the entire string of observances required in a sraaddha. A person who is not well-to-do or unwell can skip certain steps in a sraaddha with no fear of dosha or fault.

In fact people who do not have income of any kind are even permitted to do 'hiranya' sraaddha. This is the process that has just one step viz., offering rice, banana (vegetable) and a token amount by way of dakshina to the Brahmin. Thus the Sastras have a way out for all economic exigencies – such is the greatness of our elders who have prescribed the manuals so thoughtfully.

Aptitude and attitude

People who have the means and facilities to do the sraaddha properly are however urged to do it without blemish. If you have the aptitude, let not negative attitude stand in the way of your performance. Let us now see what a full performance of sraaddha entails.

1. Paarvana Homa
2. Clean, tasty and hot food
3. *Vastra* for the Brahmins called for the function and for the Acharya (the Purohit who conducts the function)
4. Dakshina for the Brahmins after bhojana (the lunch)
5. Sambhavana for the Acharya

It is considered beneficial and appropriate if an article in silver and a white silk vastra (venpattu) are offered. Quality of the items being served and articles being offered in dana should be superior and not casually made or bought.

A strange argument is made by some well-to-do people when the Purohit asks them to offer vastra – that "it is not in their family tradition". Are these persons doing everything their ancestors did? And are they eschewing everything else their ancestors did not do? It is easily possible that their elders were not as affluent as they are, and so could not offer *Vastra*. The painful aspect of such stands taken by people is that the same persons follow new modes of living, buy and use modern appliances like laptops, mobile phones, etc., and adopt styles of behaviour without any question or demur but put forward petty objections only when it comes to religious observances.

Sastras have been handed down to us via the Brahmins and Acharyas; let us listen to them and follow their directions to the extent possible without debate. If we do this future can indeed be very bright for us.

The wife's role

The Karta's wife, or the first lady of the house, has a vital role to play in the effective conduct of the Sraaddha. Her total cooperation is indispensable. It is not enough if the Karta wants the Sraaddha to be done well: his wife's active interest is even more crucial. Indeed we see in many homes that the Karta is not too concerned about doing a thorough job, but his wife, with a mix of love, insistence and sheer willpower, manages to get him do the job competently. Such homes and such women will reap rich rewards in this world and in the hereafter. **Hindu Dharma literally revolves around the lady of the house –** there is no gainsaying this truth.

Can the sons join together to do the Sraaddha?

When the sons of a deceased father or mother are living apart, each son has to perform sraaddha for his parent individually. Their doing it together is not acceptable. A joint family can of course do a joint sraaddha (but even here it is said that if the kitchens are separate it is not considered as a joint family). In a house where the sons live together the younger brothers can join up and the eldest son will perform the sraaddha. (One exception that the tradition provides to this rule is that when the mother is alive, the father's sraaddha can be done by all sons together with the son with whom she is living.) That said, it is worth noting the fact that pitrus can be at several places at the same time and will in fact be far happier if the sraaddha is individually done with homa by all the families obliged to do the karma.

Sraaddha, as noted earlier, requires complete involvement. Sastras provide a number of exceptions for economic, geographic or other kinds of compulsions – but there is no exception for *sraddha (concentration)*, and Sraaddha performed indifferently or with untimely haste is not acceptable.

Samaradhana on the day of Sraaddha?

It is claimed by some that by doing *anna dana* (donation of food) or a big offer of money to a charitable or educational institution they have successfully complied with their sraaddha obligations. Nothing can be more absurd. First of all this is the day that you devote to invoke your pitrus, remember them and pray them for your family's wellbeing. It is therefore questionable if feeding someone else on this day is even proper. You can of course augment the due observance of a Sraaddha with poor feeding in the evening of the same day or the offer of a donation to a noble cause – that is certainly a laudable gesture. But substituting such an action for sraaddha is out of the question. If you have the wherewithal and are not otherwise inconvenienced, you should definitely do the sraaddha on the date, at the time and in the manner specified.

Important do's and don'ts

- During the course of the sraaddha there should be no playing of music (even devotional songs), no small talk or political debates and no gossip. It is believed that these types of activities put off the pitrus who might decide not to grace the occasion and may go back.
- The food should be cooked at home, preferably by the lady of the house. Nothing that is prepared on a previous day –including sweet or savoury items – should be used on the sraaddha day.
- In some houses the food is prepared as if for a samaradhana, using coconut etc. This is permitted – the satisfaction of invitees is important, and it is likely that such food will appeal to them. This should however be done only with the approval of the elders in the house. Of course vegetables and other items that are not to be used in sraaddha cooking should be strictly eschewed. The food should be a fine balance between what is tasty and what is admissible.
- The ladies who cook and serve the food should be clean and dressed in *madisar* (nine-yard sari worn traditionally), and women having periods should stay away from the function.
- Food should be served hot. The serving should be professional and replete with hospitality. The Brahmins should be offered second helpings of side dishes and other items. However the food should not be thrust on them, and once they say 'enough', the serving should stop. Polite and cheerful serving of hot and tasty food goes a long way in making the sraaddha a complete success.
- The preparations should necessarily include items made of wheat, black gram, *payaru* and Gingely oil.

- *Pitru sesha:* The Karta and his brothers and sisters, sons, daughters and grandchildren and his *sapinda jnatis* are allowed to eat 'sesha' i.e. the food served after the brahmins have had their fill. A person is also permitted to eat Sraaddha food at his in-laws' place and at his maternal uncle's house.

- Even persons not in the practice of sandhyavandana should compulsorily do trikala (three times) sandhyavandana on the Sraaddha day.

- The Karta should never ask any of the brahmins if the food is tasty or if they are relishing it.

- Black *til* is a mandatory item in the list and is usually made in the form of til balls. Please note that the til item should never be picked using the thumb and forefinger.

- Except the fruits and oil-fried food nothing should be served by hand: the ladle or spoon should be used. Salt should not be served separately. The karta should not eat till the sraaddha is over, and after the lunch he should fast for the rest of the day. Pitru sesha is eaten by some at night – this is not correct. Exceptions are however made for people with health problems, who may take some liquid food at night.

- Sraaddha karma should be commenced after doing *madhyahnika*. If the karta intends to give *krusaram*, he should take his second bath (called sraaddhanga snana) only after doing so.

- 'Madi' or purity is vital for a Sraaddha. Only vastras washed and dried that morning should be worn.

- If a person who can chant '*Abhisravana*' is not available, the karta can chant suktadi, Puranas and slokas while the brahmins are having bhojana.

- *Kolam* should not be drawn on the sraaddha day, nor should puja bell be used. Anger, haste and any kind of rash behaviour should be completely avoided.

- The Karta would do well to abstain from talking to unrelated people or even reading letters etc, till he finishes the sraaddha bhojana, to the extent feasible.

- Steel vessels are not to be used in a Sraaddha.

- *Kati sutra* and *panchakachcham* are essential for a brahmin and are known to have great value and benefit for him. These should be worn at least on the sraaddha day.

- The daily *nitya puja* should be done after completion of sraaddha (for Vaishnavites there is some variation).

- If the Karta has completely forgotten sraaddha day and is reminded after the date has passed, he should perform it in the immediately following *Krishna paksha*, on the 8th day (ashtami), 11th day (Ekadasi) or the new moon day (amavasya). He should give *prajapatya krusaram* before he starts the sraaddha process.

- If the karta is too unwell to perform the sraaddha he can get it done by someone else who is capable (it can even be his son).

Gaya Sraaddha and Pratyabdika Sraaddha

An opinion doing the rounds of late is that once we do a Gaya sraaddha the annual pratyabdika sraaddha is not required to be performed. This is wrong and quite contrary to the Sastras. This is like saying we don't need to eat at all for the rest of our lives once we have eaten a magnificent feast at a five-star hotel.

Gaya Sraaddha is a memorable, once-in-a-lifetime function that every one of us must try and do, but that has no connection to the annual ritual of sraaddha, and can never take its place.

Aupasana Agni

Aupasana Agni (a prayer with homa) is part of our nitya karma, our daily prayer. This is a fact most of us have forgotten. Sraaddha gives us the one annual opportunity to do Aupasana Agni; and if we do sraaddha also in the hiranya fashion, we run the risk of becoming totally bereft of Agni and the blessings of the Agni Bhagwan, Fire God.

This is a situation that we should take care to avoid, and this is one solid reason why we should not adopt shortcuts for sraaddha but do it fully and with homa. Even if the Karta is a Brahmachari, he can perform in the Samida-dana Agni.

The right Sutra

Getting the Purohit who can perform the sraaddha according to one's own sutra would be ideal, but it is perfectly valid and acceptable if, for reasons of non-availability, one does the ritual with the Purohit of a different sutra. Abstaining from sraaddha for this reason is inexcusable.

On the subject, it is also in bad taste to vilify or criticise the Purohit who conducts the sraaddha. He is our guru and should be given nothing but respect.

Sambhavana

This is a related subject, also arousing much heartburn. Some people are fond of saying "our father used to give only so much, the Purohit is now demanding too much".

Is the cost of living not applicable to the Purohit as much as it has affected you? The acharya is to be placed on a pedestal and given freely and happily whatever we are capable of giving.

The Brahmanartha Brahmins

Another favourite pastime of some people is denigrating

Brahmins who come for 'Brahmanartha' or the Sraaddha Bhojana. As Brahmins every one of us is actually obliged to eat Brahmanartha – this is the religious reality. How many of us do, or can even think of doing it? If we shy away from this karmic duty, what right do we have to deride someone who does it as a service? Without them our Sraaddha karma would in fact be incomplete. Let us therefore revere such Brahmins and show them genuine hospitality.

Postponement

As already discussed, Sraaddha should not be postponed at our will. It should be done on the same day (month, paksha and tithi) every year. However, if theettu (tainted period) comes it should be performed the very next day when the quarantine goes off.

Vaidika rituals

If we want to regenerate belief and faith in Vaidika rituals, the only way is by respecting and trusting the Vedic scholars, comprising the acharyas, the Purohits and the performing brahmins.

The niyamas – ritualistic disciplines – handed down to us have tremendous significance for our wellbeing: let no one have any doubt on this score.

****

CUSTOMS & VALUES - FAQs

Vrata (Penance)

Qn. What are the common do's and don'ts when we observe Vrata, penance?

Ans. The word 'vrata' underscores determination, firmness in what we are doing. First we should look up the specific actions that accompany a particular penance and make sure we perform all those actions. Generally, during a vrata period, we should avoid drinking water frequently, sleeping in the afternoon, chewing paan, and cohabitation. The mind should constantly dwell on the Devata for whom the vrata is being observed. A proper guide is a must.

Qn. What do we achieve by observing vrata?

Ans. We will talk about two vratas that are usually observed: bhook vrata (fasting) and mauna vrata (observing silence.)

Fasting: The purpose of fasting as a vrata is not just to starve oneself. This vrata is symbolic of self-control. We all know that food is a major weakness of humankind; and it is this weakness that is targeted and overcome when we fast. Apart from improving the physical fitness of a person, this vrata helps develop purity of the mind and the soul and even divine powers.

Observing silence: This vrata focuses on spiritual growth of the person and is essential for spiritual aspirants. Once the mind is controlled through mauna vrata, one becomes more benign, friendlier and eventually stronger spiritually and closer to God. Ramana Maharshi says about this mauna vrata:
Mauna is the speech of self.

A word of caution: in either case, the vrata should be undertaken after getting proper guidance from a competent Guru for the desired results.

Namaskara (Obeisance by prostration)

Qn. In doing namaskara to elders are there any procedural requirements?

Ans. Yes! Obeisance is not to be done to a person who is sleeping, or performing a japa, or wearing a wet cloth. 'Abhivadana' is not to be said to ladies, but the mother is an exception. Obeisance to a sanyasi and in a general congregation is also to be done without abhivadana. In the precincts of a temple, obeisance to human beings is to be avoided.

Obeisance by males to God has to be a 'Sashtanga namaskara'. The scriptures say "Dandavath Pranameth" – meaning he should prostrate like a stick without support, flat on the stomach, indicating to God that this body is not mine, this is given by You and I surrender it to You now. For women obeisance should be a 'panchaanga namaskara'.

Above all, obeisance should be done with no thought about yourself, about whether the posture looks nice, or how others watching you are impressed. There should be no shyness, no hesitance. And no showing off.

Atma Pradakshina (Revolving on one's axis)

Qn. Is Atma Pradakshina, or rotating on one's axis, a valid substitute for doing a pradakshina?

Ans. No. In fact, Atma pradakshina does not seem to be prescribed anywhere in the Sastras except during sandhya vandanam. When it is not possible to do pradakshina, you can just do a namaskara. Doing an Atma pradakshina requires you to turn your back on the deity, which in my opinion is not seemly.

Vishnu Sahasranama

(Chanting of 1,008 names of Mahavishnu)

Qn. Is Vishnu Sahasranama a book? Or is it an advice by someone? Who conferred this upadesa and on whom?

Ans. Vishnu Sahasranama is a part of Mahabharata, like Bhagavad Gita. It was the upadesa by Sage Bhishma to Yudhishtra with Lord Krishna looking on with approval.

Qn. Is it sufficient if one were to chant "Sri Rama rameti rame raame manorame, sahasranama tattulyam Ramanama varaanane" in place of Vishnu Sahasranama?

Ans. This is a wrong concept. The sloka you have quoted is a powerful one and proclaims the greatness of Sri Rama, and can be chanted instead of the complete Sahasranama when you are rushed or you are otherwise unable to do the full chant. But to get the full benefit, one should chant the complete Vishnu Sahasranama. There is no substitute to Sahasranama.

Apradakshina (Doing the rounds from right to left)

Qn. An astrologer in our town says we should go around Navagrahas and some other deities in the reverse and not the regular pradakshina order. Is this correct?

Ans. No. Our tradition is that any deity in a temple including Navagrahas should be gone round in the regular right-to-left order and not the other way. If you hear any other view, consult your elders and decide.

Sandalwood paste

Qn. What are the points to be noted (in applying sandalwood paste on the body)?

Ans. Women should apply sandalwood paste only on the neck. It is not in our custom for ladies to apply it on the forehead. Men on the contrary should wear it only on the forehead and not on the neck. We also see men applying sandalwood paste on the chest and hands after food, but this is more out of hospitality after a feast or a bhojana. It is in our *sampradaya.*

Qn. But in Kerala it is seen that most women wear sandalwood paste on the forehead.

Ans. This is as per the regional practice, otherwise called *desaachara.* Over the centuries some of the customs have evolved and changed depending upon the region. Thus in Kerala women do not tie their hair but keep the tress flowing openly. Again the practice of ladies covering the front with a 'dhavani' (half-sari) is not followed there.

These practices are exclusive to the region and should not to be followed in other places, where the common law is to be the guide. In fact, many old and questionable regional practices are being given up in favour of common practices.

Deepa (Lighting the lamp)

Qn. Which oil can be used to light the Puja lamp at home?

Ans. Gingely oil (til oil) can be used, and if you can afford it, ghee. But groundnut oil should not be used.

Non-Resident Brahmins

Qn. I live abroad. Can I perform my 'pitru karmas' here itself, or should I come to India? Will it give me the same benefit if I do them here?

Ans. Undoubtedly, sraaddha and other such pitru karmas are best done in India, but these can be done abroad at least to keep in touch with our tradition. Moreover, fixing of the date does create some difficulties, and some observances may be impossible in foreign countries. But it is preferable to do the karmas with suitable modifications abroad, rather than abstain. The benefits will certainly accrue to some extent.

It is important that on the day of the observance one is pure and untouched by the usual domestic matters.

When you plan a trip to India you should fit in as many observances as you can during your stay.

Apara Karmas are nevertheless to be done only in India.

Vibhuti (Sacred ash)

Qn. Which is correct – applying damp vibhuti or dry vibhuti?

Ans. Generally vibhuti is to be worn damp, after making it into a paste. But when we get Swami Prasada in temples we should apply it as it is, dryly. Vibhuti that we bring from temples should not be mixed with the stock at home.

Important: After applying vibhuti paste, you should not wash the hands but cleanse it by applying the remnant on other parts including legs and hands.

Madisaar, Panchakachcham (Formal religious dress)

Qn. Please elaborate on special dresses like madisar and panchakachcham that we have to wear on religious occasions.

Ans. There is an error – though it is understandable – in your question. Madisar and panchakachcham are NOT special dresses! We are supposed to be wear these daily. And there was a time when these were being worn as a way of life. They have now become rare through the ravages of time.

At least on days of religious observances you should wear madisaar (women) and panchakachcham (men). The karmas can never be complete without it. And it is no major rocket science to put on either of these dresses, mind you – just a question of learning and practice.

On the subject of proper dressing, I must mention a related point. It has become customary to wear pants and churidars for any outing, and I see nothing wrong in that in the changed times. But when going to temples or for Veda parayana or to go to Acharya Swamigal and religious gurus for darshan, we should make it a point to go in our traditional dresses.

Madi, Achara (Sanctity)

Qn. We live in a single bedroom flat and so are unable to fully observe madi and achara. What do you suggest?

Ans. Your difficulty is understandable. Try to do the best you can, and take extra care on important days like days of pitru karma or a religious function. Since you have recognised the problem, you will surely find a solution – as they say, where there is a will, there is a way.

Dana-Dharma (Donations)

Qn. Do the words dana and dharma denote the same meaning–donating?

Ans. No, they do not. Dana is something which is given for a particular purpose, like a boon that we seek or absolution for some error we have committed. It is not a general act either: generally it is prescribed and given to a particular person on a particular occasion. And mostly the substance to be given as dana will also be specified. Dana is pre-eminent in pitru karmas.

Dharma is pure philanthropy. It is giving with no motive, no specifications, and no restrictions. No expectations either. Anyone can do dharma at anytime – in fact one should do it the moment one thinks of it, with no delay.

Sahasranama and Women

Qn. Can Vishnu sahasranama be chanted by women?

Ans. Yes, there is no restriction on chanting of Vishnu sahasranama by women. In fact, it can be chanted by all the four categories of people and not just Brahmins.

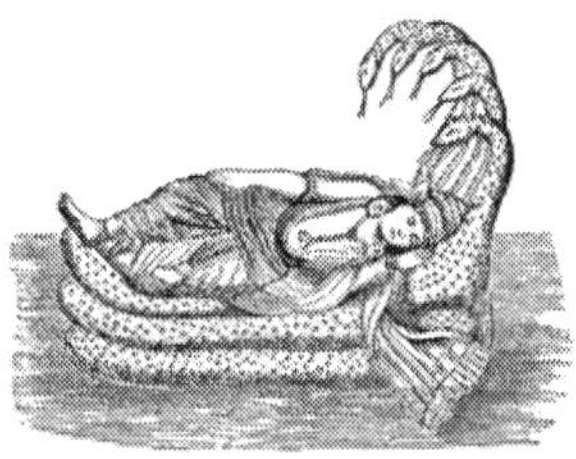

The only condition, if you can call it one, is that it should be chanted only after it is properly learnt from the right acharya.

Daily chanting of Vishnu sahasranama is highly recommended.

Puja articles

Qn. What particular care is required in sourcing materials for conducting special pujas or homa at house?

Ans. Good question. After getting the list of articles to be used for the puja or homa, please take note of the following simple rules. You will get the desired results:

1. Do not postpone the buying of puja material or dana articles (items to be donated) till the last minute. Do the purchase as early as you can.

2. Pay attention to the quality of the articles. Do not be guided by the misconception most people have, viz. 'after all, is God going to actually use the stuff?" Also do not buy cheap items for dana, as it is only to be given away. Thus for instance the rice you buy should be of a higher class than what you use for daily use in your food, or at least the same class - but not lower.

3. Again, quantity should not fall short - even a bit of excess is recommended.

4. If any article is not available consult the Purohit for advice. He is sure to get it for you or suggest an alternative.

5. On the day of the function the material should be neatly organised in the place where the puja or homa is to be conducted, at least half-an-hour before the Purohit arrives.

6. Make the purchases with devotion: let there be an element of bhakti even in this simple task.

Nitya Puja (Daily Worship)

Qn. Please elaborate on specific procedural requirements when we perform daily worship.

Ans. As far as possible, nitya puja (worship at home) should be performed with pictures, and idols are not required. It is not advisable to buy and keep puja equipments that have now proliferated indiscriminately. These equipments – called yantras – are powerful and need elaborate and intricate process manuals to be followed for using them correctly. Not all of us can do it, and so it is sensible to avoid these in performance of daily worship. Pictures are more than enough.

Of couse Panchayatana and Salagrama aradhana are altogether different. These have to be done as prescribed.

For nitya puja after sandalwood paste is made it should be collected without use of the thumb. After use the sandalwood roller and base should be kept separately and not one on top of the other. Women should not make sandalwood paste.

Likewise, women should light the lamp and extinguish it when it has to be put out.

Daily worship in the house should not be at the cost of the other domestic duties of the man or the woman. It is not right to let every other task suffer while one does puja for hours on end. Special pujas or religious functions are different – then one can give it total attention to the exclusion of domestic duties, but at least everyone else is forewarned.

Qn. Can the daily puja be performed by the lady of the house in the absence of the man?

Ans. Yes. But the Sastras have not provided for performance of 'panchayatana' pujas by ladies. But what matters is the devotion, and the continuance of puja without a break. The lady can perform the puja after removing the nirmalyam, the old flowers, and putting fresh flowers on the Gods, chanting slokas she knows. Naivedya and karpura harati can also be performed by the women.

Qn. If 'madi' vastra (dress that has not been touched after washing) is not available for nitya puja, can one use vastra that has been washed, folded already and kept separately?

Ans. Yes. But the vastra should be sprinkled with water after chanting 'pranava', and shown to the Sun God (Surya rasmi) before wearing it for the puja. But this arrangement is only for Deva karya. For pitru karma absolute madi is essential.

On the subject, a wet vastra is not to be worn while doing puja or japa. If you have no alternative, you can use a wet vastra after stirring and flourishing it seven times.

Archanas in Tamil

Qn. Can archana be done in Tamil?

Ans. Yes. Why not? No God will object. However, in a temple built on the lines of Aagama Sastra, where traditionally archana has been done in Sanskrit, who are we to make changes? Likewise when any Vedic prayoga is to be performed in a particular manner, using Sanskrit as prescribed by Rishis, we have no right to change it. Archanas in Tamil are perfectly all right where Aagama Sastra or Sastra prayoga has not been prescribed.

Sanskrit

Qn. Can anyone learn Sanskrit?

Ans. Yes, anyone can learn Sanskrit. In the olden days everyone learnt and spoke in Sanskrit in India, cutting across categories.

While on the subject, it is interesting - and also sad - to note that people think Sanskrit is a very difficult language to learn. Far from it! It is only the method used to teach Sanskrit that gives one the feeling that the language is tough. Translation and grammar are the focal points of Sanskrit teaching even in the Universities, and this may not be correct. Grammar is a must no doubt but that should not be the basis of learning to speak and write a language. Similarly, the teaching of Sanskrit should be started right from the start of education of the child and not midway.

Mahalayam

Qn. I would like to know the details of Mahalaya Paksha and related observances please.

Ans. A 'paksha' is 15 days. When the Sun enters 'kanya rasi' (Virgo) in Krishna paksha, the period is termed as 'Mahalaya paksha'. It is said that our ancestors get Yama's permission and descend from Pitru loka during Mahalaya paksha, and receive with satisfaction the offerings of their progeny. So persons who have lost their father should perform 'Mahalaya sraaddha' on at least one day during the paksha. It can even be done in the hiranya format, a simplified method with offering sambhavana and feeding of Brahmins. This is also the only paksha where we get an opportunity to offer 'tarpana' even to the departed souls of our choice, other than our own pitrus. This is known as 'karunyaka pitru tarpana'. For instance, we can do it for persons who died without issues.

Go Puja / (Cow Worship)

Qn. Can women do Go Puja (worship cows)?

Ans. Yes, they can. The power of the cow in Hindu religious rites is unparalleled. Hindu religious tracts state that the cow has features of all Gods and Goddesses. Done with faith and total devotion, cow worship can solve many problems that one may face, and grant wealth and prosperity.

Puja Bell

Qn. Is it necessary to ring the puja bell when karpura aarti is shown?

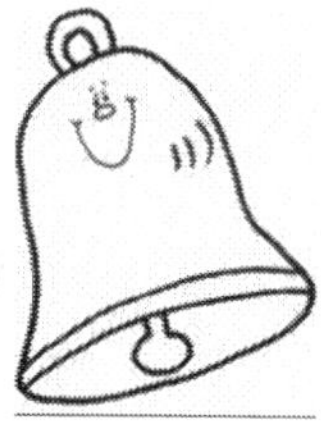

Ans. No, not really. It has however come into practice and there is nothing wrong in doing so. At the time of naivedya, the puja bell should be rung.

Remarriage

Qn. I would like to have your opinion on women remarrying after being widowed or divorced.

Ans. Generally people do not ask the same question when it comes to men. Perhaps the reason is that the Sastras do not approve of women remarrying. Again, divorce is a sin, and there is no place for it in our dharma. However, in the present day and age, when a lone woman does not have the kind of protective system that was available in the olden days in the form of many brothers and other relations, she may remarry if she feels it is justified. But such remarriages should not be conducted with vaidika rituals.

Snana (Bath)

Qn. The bath is a daily affair. Are there any procedural rules for taking a bath? And what are the vidhis (rules) for Punya nadi snana (bathing in the sacred rivers)?

Ans: Yes, there are some rules to be observed while taking the daily bath.

Nitya snana (the daily bath):

- No snana without clothes
- No snana before 3 a.m. and after 6 p.m.
- No snana after pitru karma like Tarpanam and Sraaddha
- No snana immediately after a visitor leaves, but only after a little while
- Chanting of Aghamarshana sukta recommended while taking bath

Snana in Punya nadi (bathing in a sacred river):

- One should offer prayers and do achamana before stepping into a Punya nadi. Sankalpa is also recommended.
- Snana should be done against the tide of the nadi.
- Soaps and other toiletries should be avoided.
- 'Punya-prada dina' (auspicious days) for punya nadi snana are: Janma nakshatra dina (the day of the birth star), Pusa nakshatra days, Vyatipada and Vaitruti days, Amavasya (new moon days), Sundays, Tuesdays and Saturdays.

Samudra snana: Samudra snana or taking bath in the sea is generally to be avoided. Exceptions are days of eclipse and certain other occasions under the guiodance of your purohit. But in punya kshetras like Rameshwaram, samudra snana can be done on all days.

Upanayana (Sacred Thread Ceremony)

Qn. Can upanayana be performed in 'Dakshinaayana'?

Ans. Upanayana should normally be performed only in Uttarayana (6 month period from Tamil month Thai to Ani). But if a boy has not had his upanayana done even after he has reached 11 years of age, his upanayana can be done in Dakshinaayana after doing the required 'prayaschitta' (atonement or reparation). Please do not delay the function.

Qn. Our son is aged 14 and we have not yet done his upanayana. Can it be done when his age is in even number? We are also finding it difficult to get a Purohit for performing it. Please clarify.

Ans. I have answered the question already (see above). If the boy passes the age of 11, it does not matter if the age is an even number – the upanayana can be done. It should be done fast, before the boy becomes 16.

Your problem of finding the Purohit is difficult to understand – there are many in Chennai who will be happy to perform your son's upanayana. Perhaps you haven't looked properly. If you still find it difficult, I can help.

Abhisheka (Tirumanjana)

Qn. During abhisheka, some people remove their golden ornaments, get the purohit to put them on the God or Goddess and take them back after the abhisheka. Is this proper?

Ans. This is not necessary, though it is not improper. Gold has no 'dosha' (impurity) and it is a practice with some to offer their ornaments to the God or Goddess and then wearing them.

Sandhyavandana

Qn. My father-in-law keeps saying Sandhyavandana should be performed daily by all persons with sacred thread. But neither my husband nor his grandson listens to him. What do I do?

Ans. Sandhyavandana is compulsorily to be done by all persons after their upanayana. Dharma sastra declares: ***"A person who does not do Sandhyavandana is impure and is not fit to do any Vedic karma".***

Sandhyavandana is the cornerstone of all karmas. For people who say they do not have time to do it daily, I would recommend that they could do the crucial parts to start with. The key actions in Sandhyavandana are Pranayama, Maarjana, Arghya, Praasana, Aikyanusandhana (Surya dhyana), Deva tarpana and Gayatri japa.

All these together would not take more than 15 minutes and these are easy to learn. Once a person does these regularly he will get excited and slowly move towards doing the full thing.

Anyone interested in restarting Sandhyavandana may approach me for a booklet I have written on the subject. This book is in two languages viz., Tamil and English. Kindly write to me and I will send the booklet.

Some people get satisfaction by going to the temple instead of doing Sandhyavandana. Some say they regularly participate in devotional programs like bhajans. These and other such programs, though good, are no substitutes for Sandhyavandana. There is NO excuse for not doing it.

The format for Sandhyavandana evolved by our great Rishis is very great and it contains several Veda mantras. Some portions are:

1. Purification: This covers four parts.

a) Achamana

b) Pranayama

c) Praasana

d) Prokshana

These steps are essential for condiitioning the body to receive cosmic vibrations available during Sandhya period.

2. Offering Argyam

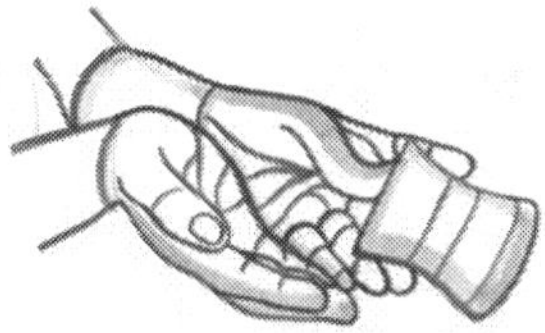

This is a way of worshipping Surya Bhagwan. This process of Argya is done with Gayatri Mantra.

3. Aikyanusandhana

This is a meditation on the identity of the self with the Supreme Being.

This particular portion of the Sandhyavandana is known as its life-line.

4. Gayatri Japa

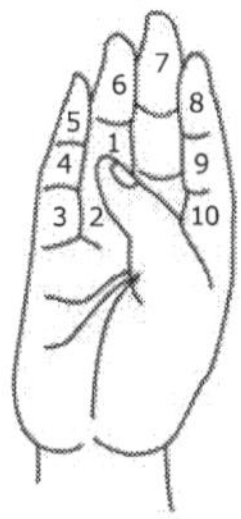

Sandhyavandana starts with purification as detailed above so that the benefits of Argya and Gayatri Japa are realised.

Timings

Q. Can Sandhyavandana be done in the morning after having coffee?

A. Yes, but it is preferable to do it before coffee. Ideally you should have had a bath as well. Otherwise after the morning ablutions, wash your hands and feet, put on the namam or vibhuti and do the Sandhyavandana. Regularity and timing are crucial to this important karma.

Vedas, Gayatri Mantra and Women

Qn. Can women learn and practise Vedas? Can women chant Gayatri mantra? I would like you to elaborate.

Ans. No, the Sastras do not permit it. Let me try to give you the rationale in some detail and related aspects of this much misunderstood subject.

The Sastras have advised women not to chant Vedas. There are a number of reasons. Before we begin, it has to be understood that Vedas are not to be equated to devotional songs or namaavalis.

- When you recite Vedas, three things are vital: the *swaras*, the *maatras* and the pronunciation. Unless these are perfect, the benefit of chanting Vedas cannot be attained. It has been established that men have the bodily and the biological structure to chant Vedas and that women do not. The nerve formation in the female anatomy is not compatible with the swaras that you have to use in chanting Vedas. The Veda swaras generated from the nabhi or the abdomen can actually harm a woman.

- Veda parayana generates great heat in the body, and this again is not conducive to the feminine nature. Besides the pronunciation that arises from 'Jataraagni' goes against the natural ethos of the female structure.

- Secondly Veda adhyayana demands that you learn from a Guru – and this is difficult for a woman.

- Though men are qualified to learn Veda, they cannot do it unless men have had upanayana samskara. And you are aware that women cannot wear yagnopaveeta.

Incidentally men from all the three varnas, viz., Kshatriyas, Vysyas and Brahmins can learn and chant Vedas – not only Brahmins.

Whether the reasons given above are convincing or not, one reason is enough. our dharma sastras do not permit chanting of Vedas by women. When we say women cannot learn Vedas, it does not mean that they should not study things like commentaries on Vedas. Even in the ancient days we come across ladies possessing good knowledge of Vedas and vedangas.

There are many powerful devotional chants like Soundarya Lahari, Lalita Sahasranama, Vishnu Sahasranama, Subrahmanya Bhujanga etc., that women can chant. In addition to these, we have slokas on deities like Siva, Lakshmi, etc. Then we have Divya Prabandha, Ramayana and Mahabharata. In addition to these, we are all aware that there are numerous bhajans and kirtanas that women can learn and practise regularly. There are several vratas exclusively for women, which are powerful. They include Chaturthi vrata, Uma Maheswara vrata, Rishi panchami vrata etc. Our worship methods include special puja-s and vratas that are exclusive for women. And for practising spiritual acts like *atma-vichara* women are equally qualified.

Hence Hindu dharma has many. many ways and means by which ladies can offer prayers.

Just because a woman cannot do a certain thing because of her natural bodily or anatomical makeup or there is no permission from our Sastras, it does not make her inferior in any way.

Finally, if despite all the points set out above that justify the proscribing of Veda chanting by women, if a lady should want to try it out, by all means let her do so. This is a free country and in Kaliyuga you can expect anything. So let us not stand in here way; Let her get the experience for herself and decide.

Rising with the lark

Qn. What is the significance of early rising?

Ans. Early rising is greatly beneficial to an individual's growth. The period approximately from 3 30 to 5 am is called 'Brahma muhurta' and is auspicious and conducive to study and learning. Religious texts tell us that the word 'Brahma' here refers to Saraswati, the Goddess of knowledge. It is therefore a well-known tenet that students and Vedic scholars as well as spiritual seekers choose this period for learning, for doing Japa and atmavichara – introspection.

Concentration levels are at their best in the serene hours before daybreak, and in any case you are advised not to be in bed after sunrise.

Vivekananda

Qn. "When a young man asks me for help to choose between Bhagwad Gita and football, I will ask him to choose football" is a saying attributed to Swami Vivekananda. Is Swamiji against Gita?

Ans. It is wrong to understand Swamiji's saying in that perspective. Far from belittling Gita, Swami Vivekananda regarded Gita as his life's guide and has exhorted people to follow its precepts on many occasions.

Coming to your question, this particular sentence, which comes midway in one of his speeches, stresses the importance of good health for young men. It is therefore important to read the quote in its context. Please read the whole paragraph around this sentence and the import will become clear.

Maharishis

Qn. Please elaborate on Maharishis in our Vedic lore?

Ans. Maharishis have discovered our Veda mantras. Though they belong to the category of devas, they are counted along with earthly human beings. They know the past, present and future, and have given mankind invaluable sutras and sastras. Kasyapa, Atri, Viswamitra, Gautama, Agastya, Rishyasringa, Vasistha, Bruhu, Jamadagni, Sanatkumara, Valmiki, Vyasa, Dadeechi are some of the well known Maharishis.

Atheism

Qn. I am not able to prove the existence of God to some persons who argue with me that there is no God. Can you give me some proof that I can show to them?

Ans. I believe in God, but I do not want to go around proving God to people who do not believe. Existence of God is to me beyond argument and if someone disputes God, it is his headache. I do not bother. It is his *praarabhda karma*.

Numerology

Qn. Are numerology and gemmology genuine sciences? Can they be trusted?

Ans. This is purely based on personal beliefs. Speaking for myself I do not believe in either, but that does not mean that people who trust these are wrong – it is their belief that counts. On the other hand astrology and horoscopes are pure sciences and can be trusted.

Dowry

Qn. Giving and taking dowry is not good and also considered a sinful act, but our Sastras seem to accept and endorse the practice. Please clarify.

Ans. It is true that Sastras acknowledge the practice of dowry being given and taken, but it should be understood that giving dowry is subject to a person's financial status and not based on the 'demand' of the bridegroom's family. People who quote Sastras to make unconscionable demands for dowry forget the following truths:

- That we get what our Karma ordains us to get, and not what we want. If it is true that one can certainly get what he aspires for, today there should no be poor man amongst us.

- That in the past, the amount and things that were given as dowry were given away by the man's family and not kept at home: this was based on the staunch belief that "we have got the gift of another family's daughter, and we should therefore match the gift with noble deeds like yajnam, dana, Brahmana bhojana and so on."

- That dowry is received only to make the giver happy and satisfied, and not to make him an unwilling pauper. Dowry should be given out of free will of the bride's family.

On this topic, you must be aware of an interesting fact of *21st Century India*: girls are so hard to get nowadays that boys' families dare not ask for dowry any more!

Naivedya / (Food offered to God)

Qn. My son asks me "why do you do Naivedya, when the God to whom you offer Naivedya is not eating anyway? After all, we only eat that food, right?" I have no answer. Do you?

Ans. Your son's question is asked even by elders out of ignorance and confusion. 'Naivedya' does not mean 'offering' in the first place. It does not mean we are giving anything to God. In Sanskrit 'nivedayaami' means "I am showing you". (To be used for "giving something" in Sanskrit is 'samarpayaami'. We use only the word nivedayaami and not samarpayaami). Naivedya is done to present the food we have prepared to God and seek his blessings, so that it becomes a 'prasada' from him that we can partake of, as well as give to others.

This is the basic meaning of naivedya and not as it is often thought. There are deeper and more intricate interpretations of naivedya, which we will see later.

Medicines

Qn. is it true that we should not take medicine in public, seen by others?

Ans. Yes. Especially medicine being taken for a chronic or persisting ailment should not be taken as far a possible in public view. If possible it is good to chant *Vaidyo Narayano Hari:* whenever one takes medicine.

Similarly, information that should be kept to oneself and not divulged except for a valid reason are ones age, assets and liabilities, family secrets, dana given and any shame that has had to be borne.

Breaking coconuts

Qn. What are the rules to be observed while breaking coconuts during religious rites?

Ans. You might be aware that a rotten coconut should not be used. A coconut with the tuft should be broken into equal halves, the tuft removed and then naivedya performed.

'Sathir thengai' (smashing one or more coconuts in front of the deity, say Sri Ganesha) should be done only by men and not by women.

Pitru Karma (Ancestor's Ceremonies)

Qn. What does the expression Pitru karma include?

Ans. Pitru karma starts with the rites to be performed for 13 days following the death of the person. Then come the monthly 'masika' cermonies including *sodakumba* for twelve months, culminating in the elaborate function at the end of the first year, *Varshabdika.*The subsequent annual ceremony, called sraaddha every year, the monthly tarpana on every amavasya day, Mahalaya paksha sraaddha etc. are other parts of the Pitru karma.

Bahishtai (Periods)

Qn. If on the day of the Sraaddha the wife has periods, can the karma be done?

Ans. Sure. According to Apasthamba sutra, the husband can do the sraaddha. Of course for others who follow different sutras, the views differ.

Company Puja

Qn. I run a company and would like to know the procedure for putting up pictures of Gods and for conducting prayer.

Ans. You can hang pictures of your ishta devatas (Gods and Goddesses of your choice), wherever you deem fit. Pictures of Lord Ganesha and Goddess Lakshmi are usually included. Idols are generally avoidable, as are yantras (unless given with specific instructions by elders).

On a daily basis, you should light up the place where the Gods are, and adorn the pictures with flowers. To the extent feasible ladies should stay away from the place during their periods.

It would be a good idea to call a Purohit and do a simple archana every friday and on days of religious festivals.

National Anthem

Qn. 'Jana gana mana' and 'Vande mataram' are our national songs now, but these are of recent origin. Is there an older national song that Vedas contain?

Ans. The Vedas contain a beautiful hymn that probably had the status of a national anthem. I am referring to the section that begins *"Aabrahman braahmano brahma varchasee jaayataam".* The meaning is as follows:

"May this country have people who are learned in the Vedas and who shine with brahma tejas. May Kings rule with good armoury and increasing productivity of the land. May cows and other animals prosper. May women be modern and keep themselves up to date. May the seasonal rains be abundant and result in rich growth of crops. May all our countrymen and women live happy and prosperous lives."

Panchayatana Puja

Qn. We are not aware if our forefathers were doing Panchayatana puja. Can we start it now?

Ans. Of course. All smarthas are expected to do this daily. Panchayatana means literally 5 types of different stones without any particular shape without any formatted figures. It should be taken for the puja as it is, as we get it naturally. These five stones are taken from five different rivers. According to one custom, this puja involves Lord Siva (baana linga) in the centre, Sun God (spatika) in the southeast, Lord Ganesha (sonapatra or red stone) in the southwest, Ambal (kareeya) in the northwest, and Lord Vishnu (saalagrama) in the northeast. More recently, a small Vel (spear) of Lord Subrahmanya is being added after Maha Periyavaal blessed and directed the addition to the panchayatana puja in one of his anugraha bhashanas. The Kanchi seer while saying so also gave an explanation. *"Nowadays it has become rare that brahmins perform aupasana daily. Brahmins are supposed to worship the agni by way of this particular aupasana karma. Since Sri Subrahmanya is a jyothi swaroopam, worshipping of Vel along with panchayathana set everyday may to some extent satisfy this need".*

Here I feel it apt to quote a paragraph from "Sankara's Teachings' by Sri Atmananda of Sri Ramakrishna Mutt on the subject: "Sankara instituted the worship of all these five Gods, Sun, Ambika, Vishnu, Ganapati and Shiva all on the same pedestal. This emphasized the idea that these are not five different Gods, but they are the one God worshipped in five different forms in different parts of India. Some wrongly think Sankara taught only Jnana and had no place for Karma. Sankara held that the place of Jnana was all-important but he knew equally well that many could not give up Karma and so they should be taught the most beneficial forms of Karma. Thus it is that the Panchayatana Puja (the worship of five Gods) came into vogue in Smartha homes. The other name for this is Siva-Puja."

Kati Sutra

Qn. We usually dress boys children with Aranakayiru (a string around the body below the navel) Is this to be worn by older males as well?

Ans. Indeed yes. This is known by the name 'Kati Sutra' and should be worn by all men, regardless of age. In fact, all deva and pitru karmas should be done only with this kati sutra on.

Desire and Greed

Qn. Is it sinful to desire (for material success in life)?

Ans. No, it is perfectly human. Unless we have some basic desires we cannot live. But as one grows older, desires should be reduced. Our involvement in observing daily anushtanas and performing the karma- should be more.

One of the dangers in permitting oneself to have desires is that it breeds avarice. The line between desire and greed is thin, and it is easy to cross the line unless one is very careful. For instance if we set our heart on something but cannot get it for a long time, it slowly becomes an obsession with us. This can arouse self-deprecation, jealousy and aversion to people who have the thing. Life becomes hell, and we stop enjoying the things God has given us.

We should be satisfied that if God had willed it, he would have given it to us, and avoid hankering after something to compulsive levels. Contentment is a virtue that we need to cultivate and nurture, to prevent becoming a victim to greed.

Guru (Preceptor)

Qn. How should we regard our Guru? How should we behave with him? Some hints please.

Ans. The most appropriate approach to the Guru is complete surrender. Only with the Guru's blessing can one progress in mastering what one is learning. To get a detailed manual on guru-sishya (preceptor-disciple) relationship, please read "Guru Geethai", comprised in three chapters of Uttara kandam in Brahma Samhita, Skanda Purana. The narration takes the form of conversation. This has also been published as a book by Ramakrishna Mutt, Chennai.

Catering services

Qn. For functions celebrated at home, can we order food from outside, through professional caterers?

Ans. It is difficult to say no, because of constraints of space and people in big cities like Chennai. When you don't have enough space and enough people-power to cook at home and serve, ordering food from a catering service is inescapable.

But for specific ceremonies like Sumangali Prarthana, Sraaddha and Sri Rudra Ekadasani food should be made with complete sanctity at home and should not be brought from outside.

Piercing the ear

Qn. Nowadays we see girls piercing their ears more than one hole and wearing multiple ornaments in the ears. Is this all right?

Ans. No. According to our Sastras, having more than one piercing of the ear is considered inelegant.

Sashtiabda Poorti (60th Birthday)

Qn. Should Sashtiabda Poorti be celebrated at the beginning of a person's 60th year, or on completing 60 years? I would also like to know about the other shanti-s associated with a person's janma nakshatra (birth-star).

Ans. Sashtiabda poorti is scheduled for the date on which the person completes 60 years of age. The different shanti-s to be performed through the life of a person can be seen in the following table.

Age	**Shanti**
One year old	Abda poorthi Aayush homa
Start of 55th year	Bheema Shanti
Start of 60th year	Ugra Ratha Shanti
Completing 60 years	Sashtiabda poorthi
Start of 70th year	Bheema Ratha Shanti
Start of 72nd year	Eka Shanti
Completing 80 yrs 8 months	Satabhisheka
Completing 100 years	Poornabhisheka

- When a son is born to your son's son Prapoutra Shanti.

Of these, Bheema Ratha Shanti, Sashtiabda Poorti Shanti and Satabhisheka are well-known and performed by many. When these three functions are done, Sri Rudra Ekadasani also is usually done a part of the function. Sri Rudra Ekadasani is a *prayaschitta* karma and it is advisable to carry it out in a elaborate manner. It will do good to the entire family in addition to the individual for whom the shanti karma is intended.

Birthday parties

Qn. Celebrating birthday parties has these days become a way of life. What do you feel about this?

Ans. Generally in our tradition, there is no place for individual birthday celebrations. We celebrate birthdays, otherwise called as jayanti functions, of Gods. Sri Krishna jayanti, Sri Rama jayanti and Sri Narasimha jayanthi are some examples. The Sastras prescribe the right way to perform such 'jayantis'. Partying for our own birthdays is a recent phenomenon: on the birthday of a child earlier elders of the household would go to the temple and perform a simple archana.

However, If you feel that you should celebrate the birthday please do not follow the Western culture in doing so, You can go to a temple, or at home you can organise a Veda parayana or nama sankirtana, and devote yourself to prayer for your well-being. Especially the practice of blowing out candles is reprehensible to our Dharma. We believe in lighting lamps to celebrate something, not putting them out.

Japa (Chanting)

Qn. Can we chant Rama nama when travelling in a bus or train or driving a vehicle?

Ans. It is not advisable to do chanting when you are driving, as your concentration should be on the road and the traffic. As a passenger you can of course chant God's names, but do it quietly and without attracting attention. Make sure you remove your footwear while chanting.

Nayanmars

Qn. Generally in all ancient temples in Tamil Nadu we see sculptures of the 63 Nayanmars. Please explain in some detail who they are.

Ans. The history of Nayanmars is to be found in Sekkizhar's poetry epic named Periya Purana, also called "Thiru Thondar Purana". This treatise is truly a jewel, comprising spirituality, devotion and service. The unusual feature of Periya Purana is that it talks about people born in diverse castes and sub-castes, with the common purpose in life of Siva's worship and service. Called 'Sivanadiyars' the Nayanmars hail from very different professions, including potters, hunters, farmers, doctors, traders, cobblers, fishermen – as well as Brahmins .

Though it is generally known that there were 63 Nayanmars, actually there were more.

The Peria Purana which speaks of Nayanmars is originally in verse. Now many publishers have brought it in prose format. Anyone pursuing the Bhakti marga should compulsorily read Periya Purana. The mindset of service to mankind will get strengthened a lot when we go through the lives of the Nayanmars.

Hearing the treatise as a Upanyasa (a discourse) is an even better method of getting its essence into our system and into our lives.

Vaidyanatha Deekshiteeyam

Qn. Please give me the details of "Vaidyanatha Deekshiteeyam"

Ans. Sri Vaidyanatha Dikshitar, born in Kandramanickam town in Thanjavur district of Tamil Nadu about 350 years ago, has given us the rules relating to Dharma Sastras as learnt by him from his Sutrakaras, in six sections. This book is known as Vaidyanatha Deekshiteeyam. Vedic vidwans treat this as a definitive manual. This work contains 6 sections.

- Varnashrama dharma
- Aahnika kaandam
- Aasoucha kaandam
- Sraaddha kaandam
- Prayaschitta kaandam
- Tithi Nirnaya kaandam

Display of love

Qn. How to display love? How does one do this properly?

Ans. Showing love is when you reach out to others with your heart, and with no self-oriented motive. This is easier said than done, especially in this day and age, when selfishness abounds and one does not reach out to others unless it is necessary. One has to consciously train the mind to develop this approach and to display genuine selfless love. It calls for effort as well.

An even more depressing thing one notices nowadays is our behaviour with relatives: we may help total strangers but will not lift a finger for our own relatives.

Parishechana

Qn: Is Parishechana to keep ants and insects away?

Ans. "Parishechana is for keeping ants and other insects around the plate. But some people out of ignorance do it even when eating on a table." This is wrong. The tradition of parishechana is a part of our bhojana vidhi, it has a spiritual intent. The ritual contains Abhidana, Gayatri, Pranahuti and other mantras with specific purpose and significance.

Mudra-s during Homa
(Finger formation during worship with fire)

Qn. While doing Homa, the fingers are kept in different formations at different times. What are the rules for this practice?

Ans. The finger formations used during a homa are called 'mudras'. The mudra gets changed with the, material used for the homa. There are three kinds of mudras:

- When ghee is used, the 'mrugee' mudra is to be adopted. Here your middle finger and the ring finger with the thumb.
- When performing homa with samit, the 'hamsee' mudra is used. Here all fingers are used except the little finger.
- When havis, rice, is used for the homa, the 'vaaraahee' or 'sukaree' mudra is practised, using all the fingers in a contracted form.

Damaged Cots

Qn. It is said that a broken cot should not be kept at home. Is this true?

Ans. In general, it is not advisable to keep broken or damaged articles in the house. It is believed that Lakshmi does not visit a house where such articles are needlessly stored.

Pradakashina (Doing the rounds in a temple)

Qn. While doing pradakshina in a temple, who should lead – the husband or the wife?

Ans. The husband should go ahead of the wife while doing pradakshina. This is also applicable when you do pradakshina of a homa or where Veda chanting is conducted.

Restlessness

Qn. The mind is restless and totally out of control. Can I meet you personally and address this issue?

Ans. You don't need to visit me for this purpose. Do daily chanting of Vishnu Sahasranama, and also write 'Sri Rama Jayam' at least 108 times every day. Whenever you get time go to a Subramanya Swami temple. Your mind will automatically settle down.

Satabhisiheka (80th Birthday)

Qn. 'Satabhisheka' is the name given for the 80th birthday celebration, but the word 'sata' means 100 – how is this correct?

Ans. 'Sata' does not only mean 100 – it also means 'abundant' or 'replete'. The occasion also marks the sighting of 1,000 moons by the person. Hence Satabhisheka shanti karma is celebrated at the completion of 80 years and 8 months, by which time the person would have sighted 1000 moons. The Sutras actually state that Satabhisheka is to be done when one completes 100 years of age, but the Shanti treatises have ruled that it should be done for the person who has sighted 1,000 moons (equivalent to 80 years and 8 months).

Blessed are those couples who are fortunate to be together when the husband has reached 80 years. Such couples are worthy of the respect given to God. Their progeny should celebrate the occasion in a fitting manner and take their blessings.

Kutthu Vilakku (The multi-face lamp)

Qn. For doing the daily puja at home, how many faces of the kutthuvilakku should be lit?

Ans. For daily puja (nitya puja) the custom is to light only one face or mukha, not more. The face that is lighted should be east or north facing. Only on special puja days, all faces should be lit.

Whenever the kutthuvilakku is lit, apply saffron on the frontage of the house and do namaskara. When the time comes for putting off the kuthuvilakku, one has to do namaskara before doing so.

The Tulsi leaf

Qn. Please elaborate on the Tulsi leaf and its significance in our religious actions.

Ans. The tulsi leaf is a multifaceted item in Hindu rituals and worship.

- A garland of tulsi leaves is the preferred adornment for Vishnu and Anjaneya.
- Tulsi leaves are ideal for archana, and as a garland for Vishnu.
- Having a tulsi maada (a tulsi tree set inside a simple construction) brings benevelonce to a house, and ladies of the house would benefit greatly from lighting a lamp at the maada and doing pradakshina-namaskara every day.
- The leaves of a tulsi tree should neither be plucked by women, nor after puja has been conducted at the maada.
- After madhyahnika and on Dwadasi day tulsi leaves should not be plucked.
- Tulsi leaves are not to be cast into a homa.
- It is considered propitious to use tulsi during naivedya, and while paying the Purohit, you can add a few Tulsi leaves.

Punya Tirtha Yatra (Pilgrimage)

Qn. Can pilgrimage be undertaken by a substitute?

Ans. Yes. To assist a person who is incapacitated, someone else may undertake his pilgrimage after taking the appropriate sankalpa (oath). Substitution is permitted for pradakshina namaskara, girivalam etc.

Yoga for Women

Qn. Can women practise yoga?

Ans. Certainly. In fact it is essential now. Gone are the days when the daily chores of a household like grinding, mixing, washing and old-style cooking automatically became a form of yoga for women and they needed no other exercise.

But women interested in practising yoga should learn from the guru and decide which yogas are suitable for them. Daily practice of yoga for 30 minutes, without compromising one's domestic duties, is a welcome addition to a woman's agenda.

Sri Uddhava Gita

Qn. What is Sri Uddhava Gita?

Ans. Sri Uddhava Gita is gist of the conversation between Lord Krishna and one of his preeminent devotees, Uddhava. The Lord answers questions asked by Uddhava in the course of the dialogue. Bhagavata Dharma and Bhakti yoga shine through this great treatise, which should be read by anyone with religious inclination.

Sagunams (Omens)

Qn. Can omens be believed? Or is it a kind of meaningless faith?

Ans. I believe in omens. I think they indicate in some way what is going to happen. As far as I am concerned these have significance and they are not meaningless.

Dog at Home

Qn. It is said one should not grow dogs at home. Is this right?

Ans. Yes. Mahabharata also states: "Dogs, broken utensils and broken cots are not considered auspicious and fit for a home" (Mahabharata Anusasana Parva 127/5).

Dharma Sastra does permit having a dog to protect our houses and agricultural lands. And it is not a crime either feeding or protecting dogs. However, it is advised that even if we have dog at home, it should be kept at a distance. Anyone who is particular about observing Vedic way of life and giving importance to religious *achara* at home should make it a point not to give a dog access to interiors of the house, and should avoid bodily contact like kissing and hugging it or taking it to bed.

It is true that people tend to develop an affectionate relationship with dogs at home and for such people it is not easy suddenly to either discontinue or do away with the habit of close contact with dogs. It will take time and effort. Feeding dogs and other animals is indeed not only a good thing to do but is our duty too.

Atharva Veda

Qn. Is it true that there are very few scholars in Atharvana Veda today?

Ans. This was true 20 years ago. Kanchi Paramacharya was seized of this problem and he took steps to proliferate Atharvana Veda. Some other eminent persons also took initiative. We have quite a few now in several parts of India who have done Atharva Veda adhyayana, and the number is growing.

Sraaddha (Death Anniversary)

Qn. On the Sraaddha tithi every year we organise Anna dana (poor feeding). Is this OK?

Ans. If you are doing anna dana in lieu of Paarvana Sraaddha, it is wrong and totally unacceptable. Sraaddha cannot be substituted with anna dana. Of course, if you are compelled to do Hiranya Sraaddha for unavoidable reasons, you can complement it with anna dana.

Pitru Shapa (Pitrus curse)

Qn. It is said that Pitrus could curse us if they are angered by our not performing pitru karma as prescribed. Are Pitrus so cruel and unsympathetic?

Ans. Let me put this in proper perspective. If a person fails to do sraaddha and the related pitru karmas he is doing something inexcusable. It has become increasingly common for people to give some lame excuse and skip sraaddha.

As to the pitrus' penchant for throwing out curses, our pitrus are not cruel. They are our own ancestors and interested in our well-being. However, even a deep sigh of sadness or annoyance of a pitru can impact our lives. And that may lead to several hardships in our families.

Golden anklets

Qn. Can women wear golden anklets?

Ans. No. It is not considered proper to wear gold below one's hip.

Vishnu Purana (The Lore of Vishnu)

Qn. Kindly elaborate on Vishnu Purana and the other Puranas.

Ans. Maharishi Paraasara, the father of Sage Vyasa, wrote Vishnu Purana. Made up of 23,000 slokas, Vishnu Purana has many a valuable description of Deva and Pitru karma-s that one has to observe.

The complete set of 18 Purana-s in the format we now know was however compiled by Sage Vyasa. The Puranas are composed in 4 lakh (400,000) granthas. The names of the 18 Puranas are:

1.	Skanda Purana
2.	Narada Purana
3.	Vayu Purana
4.	Vishnu Purana
5.	Brahma Vaivartha Purana
6.	Koorma Purana
7.	Agni Purana
8.	Linga Purana
9.	Vamana Purana
10.	Padma Purana
11.	Varaha Purana
12.	Matsya Purana
13.	Garuda Purana
14.	Bhagavata Purana
15.	Bhavishya Purana
16.	Brahmmanda Purana
17.	Brahma Purana
18.	Markandeya Purana

In addition to this, there are 18 Upa-Puranas as well.

Puttaparthi Sai Baba

Qn. I would like to know your leaning towards Puttaparthi Sai Baba and your opinion of him.

Ans. I revere him. In the three noble pursuits of Bhakti, religion and social service he and his devotees all over the world are doing a magnificent job and their work is nothing short of a silent revolution.

I would like to recount here one of his sayings that has impressed me profoundly: "So you think the person who hates you is doing a wrong. Then by hating him in return are you not doing the same wrong? You resent the disrespect shown to you by someone - how is it justified to return the disrespect? The path of love to all is the right path. Go voluntarily even to the person who does not come to you and talk to him with affection. You will then sense the fount of happiness that such unconditional love brings."

Vendudhal (Commitment)

Qn. I belong to the Vadakalai (Iyengar) sect and believe in Vedic rites. Can I make a commitment to God that I will shave off my head?

Ans. Generally, after we do the shaving off of the head in our childhood based on our family beliefs, we should never do it again. So a commitment of such a nature will have no religious recognition. Exceptions are found for those who follow Sama Veda sect.

Vetrilai Kodi (Betel Leaf Plant)

Qn. Can we, Brahmins, grow a betel leaf plant at home?

Ans. No. This is not permitted by our Sastras.

Brahminism

Qn. Does one become a Brahmin only by birth? Or can Brahminism be inculcated by the manner in which one leads one's life?

Ans. A person who is born to a Brahmin couple can be called a Brahmin. But this rule has some exceptions. A person born in a different caste can attain Brahminism because of the virtues he has achieved in his earlier births through his noble deeds. This is rare but possible.

While on the subject, I would like to say one more thing. A Brahmin by birth has been prescribed up to forty samskaras in order to attest his Brahminism and make him a true Brahmin in the full sense of the word. Of these samskaras, fourteen are known as 'niyata samskaras', meaning these are common to all:

1. Garbhaa dana
2. Pumsuvanam
3. Seemanthonnayanam
4. Jaata karma
5. Namakarna
6. Anna praasana
7. Choula
8. Upanayana
9.
10. } Veda vrata
11. }
12. }
13. Samaavarthana
14. Vivaha

Of course vivaha or marriage is not strictly niyata samskara because one may live one's life as a bachelor.

Ekadasi Vrata (Observance of Ekadasi)

Qn. I used to observe Ekadasi vrata regularly but I am not able to do so these days, as I am not keeping good health. What should I do?

Ans. Don't worry. Observance of vrata is not compulsory for persons who have problems with health, or compelling circumstances and age.

Vibhuti and Sandalwood

Qn. After applying vibhuti paste on the forehead, can we also apply sandalwood paste and saffron?

Ans. Yes, but not over the vibhuti the three lines of vibhuti should not be touched. Sandalwood and saffron can be applied as a small dot just below the vibhuti.

Rudraksha maalai (Rudraksha garland)

Qn. I wear the Rudraksha garland regularly. Are there any regulations relating to this?

Ans. If it is a single rudraksha worn as a garland tightly around the neck it can be worn all the time, and there is no need to take it off.

Otherwise, the rudraksha maalai must be taken off during sleep, ablutions, sex and while performing sashtanga namaskara.

Doing Japa

Qn. Should japa be performed holding the poonal (sacred thread) in one's hand?

Ans. No. There is no need to hold the poonal when one performs japas including Gayatri.

Tarpana timing

Qn. I am told that Amavasya tarpana and Mahalaya *hiranya* sraaddha etc. should done only at midday and not early in the morning, but it is difficult for me to find time in the day. What should I do?

Ans. We must appreciate the fact that timing was set for observance of many karmas in the olden days, probably from the standpoint of a village life. It is difficult to cope with the demands of city life. If we insist that the timings set cannot be changed, there is the danger of people dropping the karma altogether.

It is therefore far better that the tarpana is done – Sastras will definitely excuse the timing difference. Besides, if the entire population of kartas were to require the Purohit to come at the same time, how will he manage to visit all the houses within that stipulated time?

One thing though: the time set for parvana sraaddha (death anniversary) should be observed and the discipline required for its performance to be kept in mind and observed implicitly. Sraaddha is an all-powerful karma and should be done exactly as per the time, the process and your family beliefs.

A general piece of advice for such doubts: your house Purohit is the best guide and if you follow his advice you need have no qualms.

Music and dance for Vaidika family girls

Qn. We belong to a very tradition bound family. I would like to enrol my daughter in music and dance classes. Is it OK?

Ans. Music is fine, but avoid dance.

Bhakti on Television

Qn. We see a number of programs these days on TV related to religion, Godliness and Bhakti. Are these good?

Ans. Certainly – it is worth seeing such programs to reinforce our religious beliefs.

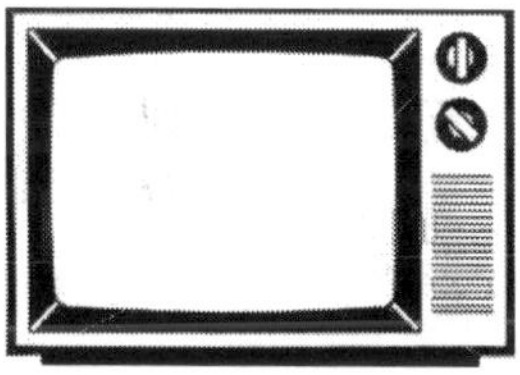

But there is an inherent danger here – we might get lulled into a sense of complacence and stop doing our nitya pujas and visiting temples. For example, the mere passive watching of a person chanting Vishnu Sahasranama on TV is not equal to chanting it ourselves.

Doing Japa standing in water

Qn. What are the rules to be observed while performing japa standing in water?

Ans. Japa should be done in knee-deep water, but Gayatri japa should be done only on the shore and not in water.

Durga Puja (Worship of Goddess Durga)

Qn. Can Durga Puja be done at home?

Ans. Yes, but it is preferable to do it in the Durga sannidhi in a temple. The prescribed routine is that it should be done every Tuesday for at least nine weeks in a temple.

Arya-Dravida race theory

Qn. It is said that the Aryan race came into India and conquered the Dravidians. Is this true?

Ans. This is pure fiction and should not be believed. The simple fact that contradicts this theory is that the religious and other customs and habits of Dravidians and Aryans were the same from time immemorial - how could that have happened, if the Aryans came from a different culture? Even well before the dates that the 'historians' give for the alleged Aryan invasion, we find the same tradition and worship methods existed with the Dravidians.

The Aryans and Dravidians belong to the same race - there is no difference. We are all Hindus. This was only a concoction by the British in their strategy to split the nation at several levels. Some of our own people propagated the theory in return for favours from the British and tried to make a major bifurcation. This has however failed and the differentiation hardly exists now.

Non availablity of Purohits

Qn. We belong to the Bodhayana Sutra, and in the area we live we find Purohits who know only Aapasthamba Sutra. How do we perform sraaddha under the circumstances?

Ans. Our sastras permit you to perform sraaddha according to a different sutra if you do not get the Purohit who knows your sutra. So please go ahead - but on no account skip the sraaddha. Pitru karma is very important and should not be postponed or cancelled.

Sumangali Prarthana (Prayer for long life of the husband)

Qn. Can Sumangali Prarthanai be done whenever we feel like doing it?

Ans. Generally Sumangali Prarthana is done in each family not more than once a year. This is not a Vedic karma but nevertheless of great significance. It should be performed with devotion and discipline, in line with the process set by tradition of the particular family.

The day has to be selected carefully, looking at the days yoga etc. and usually a Monday or a Friday is chosen.

A sidelight of this function is that some families present a six-yard sari to the 'pendugal' viz. the married lady selected as proxy for the worship. This is incorrect – it should be a nine-yard sari. It should also be remembered that the total number of sumangalis (married women) plus the kanya (unmarried girl) should be an odd number.

Colour of the Veshti

Qn. Can grahastas (married men) wear veshti in kaavi (brownish yellow / orange colour)?

Ans. No. *Kaavi vastra* is meant for Sanyasa ashram. It should not be worn by a grahasta. Even while observing some vrata, kaavi to be avoided. If there ia a need for a colour vastram, one can use a colour other than kaavi.

Ladies and Upasana

Qn. Is it wrong for ladies to wear flowers on days of Upasana?

Ans. It is perfectly in order for ladies to wear flowers and apply sandalwood paste, eye-lining etc. on the day of upasana. Adornment by the lady is not proscribed by the Sastras.

Change of Name

Qn. Recently we come across instances of people changing their names on the advice of someone for some purpose. Is this proper?

Ans. The practice of change of name is fundamentally flawed. 'Namakarana' or the naming of a person by the parents with blessings of elders at the time of one's birth is 'samskara' karma – a religious ritual – and one cannot change that name willy-nilly. You can make minor alterations when spelling out your name in English, if you have to, but no more.

Once you place your faith in God, religious observances and Sastras, there is no need for practices like numerology and other *-ologies*. Doing so will only create confusion and worry throughout our lives.

Aradhana of Siddha Purushas

Qn. Is it all right to do aradhana (worship) of great people who have attained siddhi – siddha purushas in our house?

Ans. Certainly. Aradhana mahotsavas of siddha purushas and sanyasis can be performed at home.

Pancha Gavya

Qn. Can *pancha gavya* be consumed as it is, and at any time? I would like to learn all about *pancha gavya*.

Ans. 'Pancha gavya' comprises five things related to a cow: its milk, curds, ghee, cow dung and urine. These should be assembled and consumed only to the accompaniment of the prescribed mantras. The consumption of pancha gavya should be for valid reasons and not 'just like that' (in such a case, it should be for a very small quantity). Pancha gavya is a powerful antidote for diseases and chronic ailments, infertility and poverty, and is recommended for absolution of sins and passage into the after-world. It is an integral part of some Vedic karmas too.

Ahankara (Ego)

Qn. People used to tell me that I am egoistic, but I did not heed the advice. Lately I have myself started sensing my arrogance and would like to cleanse myself. What should I do?

Ans. It is difficult not to experience *ahankara* - in fact, even saying "I have no ego" is an exhibition of ego. We can of course temper it, by yoga and dhyana.

The Sringeri Peetadhipati Sri Sri Bharata Teertha Swamigal has made a beautiful statement on this subject: *"The only way to get over ahankara is to realize and always bear in mind that there are others bigger and better than us, more educated and so on. With this mindset, a person can never become proud and arrogant."*

More often than not, your *ahankara* is seen by everyone around you but you are blind to it. This makes it tough to overcome. But in your case you have already felt it - so conquering it should be easy. Perhaps a bout of social service can cleanse you.

Picking flowers for puja

Qn. Can flowers for puja be picked from plants growing near a dirty drain?

Ans. Yes. The flower of such a plant is not tainted by its surroundings and is considered fit for use in worship.

Puja Dravya (Articles used in pujas)

Qn. How do we ensure the purity of Puja dravya or articles used in nitya puja or special pujas?

Ans. We need have no worry on this score. The Sastras aver that puja items bought in shops can be accepted as pure.

Talking of purity, Sastras also state that persons suffering from diseases, children whose upanayana has not yet been performed, and ladies working in the kitchen are exempt from any test of purity and can be accepted with no questions.

Navagrahas (The nine planets)

Qn. We are told the Navagraha devatas are all powerful, and can decide every step of our life. With everything pre-determined, why bother to put in personal effort when what will happen will anyway happen?

Ans. It is certainly true that the Navagraha devatas have a role in influencing the lives of us mortals and this is the reason for unexpected reversals as well as fortunes in a man's life. To some extent the horoscope of the person can give broad hints as to what he can expect. However this cannot negate the power of endeavour, of effort put in with zeal and devotion.

The Devata may direct your life, but your life has to be run by you – and how you run it largely decides your quotient of happiness. You can make a bad situation worse or tolerable, depending upon how well you handle it. Likewise you can muff a great opportunity with inept management or reap the richest rewards by putting in sincere effort. So do not decry human effort. I am reminded of my grandfather's words: "the Sun beats down on you mercilessly in summer, but it's up to you to use an umbrella or some such device to mitigate its impact."

Amavasya Tarpana

Qn. Is it true that for a few months after marriage, the respective parents of the bridegroom and the bride should not perform Amavasya tarpana?

Ans. No, it is not true. Tarpana should not be forgone at any time. One small amendment is that with *til*, some *akshada* (rice grains) are added. Some people use arugampul (a kind of grass) in the place of darbhai.

Gaya Sraaddha

Qn. When the elder son performs sraaddha, is it sufficient that other younger sons are just present there? It is also said if one performs sraaddha at Gaya, he is absolved from doing sraaddha thereafter. Is it correct?

Ans. If the brothers of a family live separately, either with or without partition of the family property, they have to perform sraaddha separately. Getting together on the day of sraaddha and performing one sraaddha is not acceptable. The pitrus are capable of being at several places at the same time, and will in fact be much more satisfied if sraadha is done for them by all the sons individually. If they live together in a joint family, a single sraaddha is enough.

As for Gaya Sraaddha, it is absurd to think that it exempts you from doing sraaddha for life – this is quite contrary to the sastras. This is like saying that if you have a stupendous feast at a five-star hotel one day, you don't need to eat for the rest of your life. Sraaddha at Gaya is a very fulfilling, and one should try to do it in one's lifetime. But it has no connection to the *pratyabdika* sraaddha that you have to do annually. The annual sraaddha has to be done, and there is no exception.

Suryodaya (Sunrise)

Qn. Are we not supposed to see Sunrise?

Ans. Yes. In general the Sun should not be seen rising or setting. By accident if we see sunrise or sunset, we should do worship of the Sun. Seeing the reflection of Sun in water is also to be avoided.

Silence during meals

Qn. Should one observe silence while taking meals? What are the rules to be followed, if any, while eating?

Ans. The following rules have been prescribed for proper intake of food:

1. A grahasta should not be silent while eating, except till the time of 'praanaahuti' (parishechana).
2. One should not eat wearing a wet vastra or a single vastra.
3. Lunch and dinner should be taken by males (with sacred thread) only after 'parishechana'.
4. When you have to drink water using your left hand, the right hand should be touching the leaf on which food is served.
5. After a certain age, try to avoid eating old food, except if it is related to buttermilk, milk or oil.
6. Do not criticise the food while eating. The Upanishads say so. You can mention the flaw gently to the cook after completing the meal.
7. Avoid 'paraanna' i.e., eating outside food. This is difficult in this day and age, but at least during sraaddhas and other days of vrata or other religious observances, outside food should be avoided. One ritualistic exception to eating paraanna is brahmana bhojana - when you are invited as a brahmin for a ritualistic feast.

Valentine's day

Qn: What are your views on celebrating Valentine's Day?

Ans: The very concept of Valentine's day is absurd. Young minds have been polluted and misguided into making this barbaric pratice an acceptable one. Elders object to it primarily because it propagates permissive behaviour that is alien to our culture.

Spirituality

Qn. How do I know how I am progressing in my spirituality? Is there a measurement scale?

Ans. There is no measuring scale for spirituality, no periodic examinations and no grading. A person engaged in spiritual advancement simply follows the precepts prescribed for him in his religion properly and observes the rules sincerely. The true measure of whether one has shown progress in one's spiritual or religious pursuits is when the question itself disappears!

When this happens, the person reaches a state of pure bliss and such doubts do not assail him anymore. He experiences the vastness of what he has taken on, and is truly humbled. Have the right Guru, and his blessing - you do not need to worry at all about how you are doing or progressing.

House cleaning in the morning

Qn. Please enumerate matters to be attended to while cleaning the front of the house every morning.

Ans. It is a good practice to clean the portico and anoint it with a nice *kolam* before sunrise or soon after sunrise. This is one of the practices that comes from our ancient days and is considered auspicious. {There are occasions when you should not be drawing a *kolam* - but don't stop the water-wash even on those occasions.}

The lady of the house does this usually, but men can do it as well. And draw the *kolam* on the doorstep as well. It is believed that some particular devatas stand guard for our welfare on the doorstep. Use rice flour for the *kolam*, and on special days the red clay paste has also to be applied.

Growing a beard

Qn. Is it good to grow a beard?

Ans. Growing a beard without reason is not permitted by Sastras. Even when one grows a beard during *pitru deeksha* or *garbha deeksha,* or during vratas, one should shave it after completion of the karma. (Of course, this does not apply to Sanyasis, Sikhs and some other.

Shannavati Tarpanas

Qn. I would like to learn about Shannavati tarpanas, please.

Ans. A total of 96 tarpanas have to be performed spread over in one year. This is known by the term Shannavati. After a father's sraaddha, the performance of Shannavati till the next tithi is pitru karma of great value, although not compulsory. Doing a Shannavati at least once during one's lifetime is an immensely fulfilling experience.

Shannavati is not to be done for a deceased mother when the is still alive. If the mother is alive though father is dead, Shannavati can be done.

Amavasya may sometimes coincide with the first day of the month Shannavati can be done.

The 96 days of Shannavati comprise amavasya (12), monthly sankaramanam (12), the ashtakas etc. (12), Vaidruti (13), Vyateepadangal (13), Manvadi days (14), Ugadi days (4), Mahalaya Paksha days (16).

The rules relating to combined observance should be noted carefully. Your Purohit would be able to guide you in this regard.

The Sastras state that each of the 96 can be done as a Parvana sraaddha, but since this is virtually impossible, these can be done as tarpanams.

Immortality

Qn. Hindus believe in immortality. But is it not against nature?

Ans. According to our scriptures, it is the soul which is eternal and indestructible. The immortality Hindus believe in pertains only to the soul and not the body. Sri Krishna in Bhagwad Gita asserts that *just as a man discards his old clothes and wears new ones, the soul discards the old body and enters a new one.*

Nama Sankirtana

Qn. Please brief me about Nama Sankirtana?

Ans. Nama sankirtana or chanting and singing God's names (Bhagavan-nama) brings us peace, happiness and freedom from petty worries. Each of us should cultivate the habit of daily nama sankirtana, otherwise known as bhajan with other family members at home and in community functions as often as possible. Perhaps this could be one of the reasons we find the inclusion of Bhagawan names several times in our daily Sandhyavandana too.

The joy that one experiences while doing bhajan cannot be described – it has to be experienced. However, please do not fall into the misconception that nama sankirtanam is an alternative to *nitya karma* and other karmas that one has been ordained to perform. These cannot be skipped simply because you do bhajans.

Recently I have come across someone telling that doing nama sankirtanam could be an alternative to performing Sraaddha. This is absurd. The precepts and practices given to us by our ancestors such as Bodhayana, Aapasthamba, Aasvalaayana and other Sutradhars are rare jewels and we dare not ignore these or liken them with the chanting of Bhagavan-nama. If we do so – and this is unfortunately happening more and more – the loss will be only ours.

Who is Superior - Vishnu or Siva?

Qn. I am confused. Who is the superior Lord, Mahavishnu or Lord Siva?

Ans. Mahavishnu and Siva are note different - they are the same: this is declared by Vedas and endorsed by Puranas

Sage Markandeya sings a rare hymn known as Hariharatmaka Stotra where he declares unequivocally that there is absolutely no difference between Shankara and Vishnu. The first few shlokas of the hymn are given below:

शिवाय विष्णु रूपाय विष्णवे शिव रूपिणे ।
यथान्तरं न पश्यामि तेन तौ दिशतः शिवम् ॥ १ ॥

अनादि मध्य निधनं एतद् अक्षरं अव्ययम् ।
तदेव ते प्रवक्ष्यामि रूपं हरि हरात्मकम् ॥ २ ॥

यो विष्णुः स तु वै रुद्रो यो रुद्रः स पितामहः ।
एका मूर्तिस् त्रयो देवा रुद्र विष्णु पितामहाः ॥ ३ ॥

"I salute Siva who is in the form of Vishnu and Vishnu who is in the form of Siva. I don't see any difference between the two and I pray to them that they bestow me Kalyana seeing my equality disposition. This Harihartmaka svarupa (form) is indeed the eternal and indestructible Brahman. He who is Vishnu is indeed Rudra and He who is Rudra is indeed Brahma. The same Brahma Svarupa has taken three forms based on their duties – creation, protection and destruction".

Sri Ati Rudram

Qn. Please let us know the significance of Sri Ati Rudram

Ans. The great Hindu sages have codified and given us various yagnas and homas for our day-to-day observance and to fulfil our duty towards pitrus and devas. In addition to benefiting the individual, these rituals also result in universal peace and prosperity. Sri Ati Rudram is one such yajna.

Sri Rudram, a powerful and greatly beneficial set of mantras, is found in Yajur Veda (4th kanda). Sri Rudram is recited in two sections: Namakam and Chamakam. Sri Rudram is recited during Abhisheka. During Pradosha kala it is recited in temples. Our ancestors used to recite it regularly every morning.

Maharishi Satapata in his 'Maharnava Karma Vipaka' has listed four types of procedures compatible with vedic and scriptural lore for the chanting of Sri Rudram. These are:

1. Sri Rudram
2. Sri Rudra Ekadasani
3. Sri Maha Rudram
4. Sri Ati Rudram

each being more potent than the preceding one.

1. Sri Rudram: Sri Rudram is a single recitation of Sri Rudram.

2. Sri Rudra Ekadasani: Sri Rudra Ekadasani is the recitation of Sri Rudram by 11 Vedic scholars 11 times. In addition to the Sri Rudra Parayana as cited, Rudra homa, abhisheka and archana also have to be performed as part of Rudra Ekadasani. This is also known as Ekadasa Rudram. Mahanyasam, a set of procedures with Veda mantras to invoke Lord Shiva and offer Him all the *Upacharas*, has to be done before starting Sri Rudra Parayana.

3. Sri Maha Rudram: Sri Maha Rudram is the recitation of Sri Rudram by 121 Vedic scholars 11 times. As detailed above under Sri Rudra Ekadasani, Rudra homa, abhisheka, archana etc. are also performed during Maha Rudram.
This is also a one-day program.

4. Sri Ati Rudram: Sri Ati Rudram is the recitation of Sri Rudram by 121 Vedic scholars. 11 times each day on 11 consecutive days. On all these 11 days there will be Sri Rudra homa, abhisheka, archana etc. Thus by the end of the 11th day Sri Rudram would be recited 121 x 11 x11 times in the course of a Sri Ati Rudram.

Every individual related in one way or another with Sri Ati Rudram – the organisers, the persons who do the parayana, the assistants who look into all the details, even the silent participants who come, sit and listen can consider themselves blessed and would be greatly benefited. Sri Ati Rudram is indeed a panacea for universal peace, positive energy emanating from the vibrations, and environmental wellbeing.

Veda and Vedanta

Qn. I would like to know the precise meanings of the words Veda and Vedanta.

Ans. Vedanta is a part of Veda.

As you know, the Vedas are four: Rig, Yajur, Sama and Atharvana. The main text of each of the Vedas is known as its Samhita. Besides Samhita, the Veda has two other sections: Brahmana and Aaranyaka. Brahmana contains the basic mantras, and lists the Vedic karmas and the procedure for each of the karmas. Aaranyaka is concerned with the philosophy and the fundamental meaning of each mantra in the Samhita and each Vedic karma described in Brahmana. Known as 'Gnana kanda', the final section of Aaranyaka comprises the Upanishads.

There are today ten Upanishads that are generally accepted and prevalent. These are:

Name of the Veda	Name of the Upanishad
Rig Veda	Aitareya Upanishad
Krishna Yajur Veda•	Taittiriya Upanishad Kathopanishad
Shukla Yajur Veda	Isa Upanishad Brahadaranyaka Upanishad
Sama Veda	Kena Upanishad Chandogya Upanishad
Atharva Veda	Mundaka Upanishad Prashna Upanishad Mandukya Upanishad

• Maha Narayaneeya Upanishad of Yajur Veda is also added in the count by some.

The Upanishads and Brahma Sutra together expound the philosophy of the Vedas and give out the inner meanings of the varied observances and rites. Vedanta is the name given to this part of the Vedas. Vedanta is meant for people who have imbibed all the Vedas and understood the different rituals, and have observed them implicitly, and would like to explore the secret of this great lore.

For the common person, understanding the procedures and doing them diligently and with discipline is by itself a great achievement, and he could take of study of the Vedanta after he has mastered the Vedas. In fact for such a person Vedanta would start making sense automatically.

Daily rituals

Qn. I am a married person. I would like to know about the daily rituals and observances I should maintain.

Ans. Full-fledged observance of all the rituals prescribed by Dharma Sastras in today's life-style may not be possible. But if we follow the following niyamas and rites day to day, it is not only helpful to us during our working life but can become a great foundation for a spiritually fulfilling post-retirement life. And all these are straightforward and fairly simple.

The don'ts:

- Using harsh or vulgar words and phrases and spoiling the language: the truth in your words does not permit you to be crass and strident
- Leaving a residue in a vrata or in a loan – these are torrid remainders that can burn you
- Being burrowed in ceaseless thoughts
- A grahasta wearing a single vastram, garment
- Drinking using the left hand for the cup, or eating while standing
- Doing japa, or puja, chanting Veda with no vibuti or nama on the forehead.

The do's:

- Ladies can chant Bhagavan-nama while attending to the daily routine in the kitchen.
- Men can chant Bhagwan namas while taking bath, and subsequent dressing.
- One should wash one's feet and hands after ablution and rinse at least twice
- Observance of a vrata with no dilution: it is to be noted here that one is sometimes compelled to do sraaddha bhojana (eating at a sraaddha) or take medicine on a day of fasting, or break one's silence during a mauna-vrata. These in no way affect the vrata.

Brahma Yajna during Avani Avittam

Qn. Some people say that while doing the pitru tarpana in the Brahmayajna during Avani Avittam, a person whose father is alive should not keep the poonal to his left. Some say this is OK. What is the right procedure?

Ans. First things first: Brahma yagna is a nitya karma – a ritual to be performed daily, after madhyahnika. It is not Avani avittam specific.

Coming to your doubt, the pitrus we worship in Brahma yagna are different from our individual pitrus. The pitrus for whom this tarpana is done are called nitya pitrus or divya pitrus. Without going into details, all of us – regardless of father being alive or not – have to perform the pitru tarpana segment of Brahma yagna with poonal worn in the traditional manner i.e., to the left. However, if one feels otherwise for some sentimental reasons, they can skip this portion.

Natural Purity

Qn. What do the Sastras regard as naturally pure?

Ans. According to the Sastras, the following substances are supposed to have unquestioned, absolute purity:

- Fire
- The feet of a Brahmin
- The hind part of a cow and the face of a goat or a horse
- Puja articles even if bought at a shop
- A newborn
- Mice, flies, bees and their ilk, all amphibian creatures and things, elephants and horses
- Water flowers and garlands, even if preserved in a refrigerator.

Besides, one should not question the purity of a child, a woman working in the kitchen, or a person with a disease.

Learning other than one's own Veda

Qn. I am a *Vaishnavite* belonging to the branch of Sama Veda. I have not learnt anything in Sama Veda but have learnt and memorized Yajur Veda *Purusha Sukta* etc. Is it wrong?

Ans. The Perumal *aradhana,* daily puja, is a very important aspect of a *Vaishnavite's* life. The *Suktadis* of Yajur Veda are part of the daily Perumal *aradhana* irrespective of one's Veda. So what you're doing is absolutely right. Besides, during temple worships for *Vaishnavites* the *Goshti* and similar functions are mandatory: and on such occasions the chanting of Yajur Veda in addition to *Divya Prabandha* is done. Therefore, there is no lapse on your part, and you should be happy that you are able to recite the *Suktadis.* That said you should at the earliest opportunity also learn at least a few portions of the Veda to which you belong.

Of course, for a person joining a Veda *pathasala* for Veda *adhyayana* my answer would be different. Sastras say that one should first do Veda *adhyayana* of the Veda to which he belongs, and then study other Vedas if he chooses to. Such a person should not join any other *pathasala* other than his own Veda branch.

You are in a different category and this condition doesn't apply in your case.

Veda mantra as ring tone?

Qn: Can I have a Veda mantra as my Ring tone in my mobile?

Ans: No. It is not advisable. Instead please choose some sloka for this purpose.

Sacredness of Vows

Qn. Are the vows to be perform in detail to derive benefit?

Ans. All vows have to be certainly observed in toto to be effective. The exchange between Sri Sri Chandrasekarendra Bharathi Swamigal, the Sringeri Sage, and a devotee bears this out.

A disciple who was suffering from acute skin trouble approached His Holiness for relief. His Holiness directed to go to the Temple of God Subrahmanya at Tiruchendur perform archana and do a certain number of prostrations before the Deity. He accordingly went for some Sashtis; but after the lapse of a few months he found it necessary to go to Madras and feared that he might have to miss a Sashti. In this dilemma he again sought His Holiness.

D. As ordained by your Holiness, I have been going to the Tiruchendur Temple all these months. Now I find I have to go to Madras and may not be back in time for the next Sashti. May I know what I am to do?

H. H. Is the matter urgent?

D. Yes.

H. H. Then start from Tiruchendur on the night of the Sashti, go to Madras and return to Tiruchendur before the next Sashti. You have a fornight's interval to transact your business at Madras.

D. I fear my business at Madras may require my presence there for a longer time.

H. H. Is that so? In that case, you may start from Tiruchendur the night of the next Sashti also, go to Madras, finish your business and then return in time for the Sashti next after that.

D. I desire to know whether the Sashti left out cannot be compensated by extending the period of vow by one more Sashti so that the total number of twenty-four Sashtis may have been fully observed.

H. H. There is certainly no harm in your observing a Sashti after the termination of the year of vow, but it cannot certainly be counted as included in that period.

D. Then your Holiness means that all the twenty four Sashtis must be within the year of vow?

H. H. Was that not exactly your vow?

D. It was. I have heard that there is a famous shrine of God Subrahmanya at Tiruttani (Thanikachala) near Madras. May I go to that temple on the Sashti I have to be at Madras?

H. H. Certainly. But with what purpose?

D. As an alternative to my going to Tiruchendur on that day.

H.H. We are quite incompetent to discuss about the relative merits of the sacred images of the God Subrahmanya at Tiruchendur and at Tiruttani. In cases of vows where definite benefit is expected, no alternative or substitute is permissible.

D. But, if the terms are so inviolable, what am I to do when I find myself compelled, by circumstances beyond my control, to violate them?

H.H. I quite agree. If the circumstances are so beyond your control, you can certainly do nothing. You must tamely submit to fate which places such insurmountable obstacles in your way.

D. But if I submit to that as inevitable, what becomes of my vow?

H.H. It is no longer kept. That is all.

D. God forbid. Then I shall take your Holiness' first suggestion and go to Madras twice, if necessary, without detriment to the Tiruchendur Sashti.

H.H. Do so.

Two powerful schools of thought

Qn. Can we have an idea about Advaita and Visishtadavita?

Ans. These are two significant schols of thought on the concept of Hindusim.

Advaita

While the first systematic exponent of Advaita was Gaudapada, the *Parama-Guru* of Sri Sankara, it was Sankara who brought forth Advaita philosophy in its final and perfect form. His commentary on the Vedanta Sutras, Sariraka Bhasya, can clarify the philosophy to the reader.

The teachings of Sankara can be summed up in half a verse: - *Brahma Satyam Jagan Mitya Jivo Brahmaiva Na Aparah.* "Brahman (the Absolute) alone is real; this world is unreal; and the Jiva or the individual soul is non-different from Brahman." Thus according to Sankara, whatever is, is Brahman. All differences and plurality are illusory. This is the quintessence of his philosophy.

The Atman is self-evident and needs no extraneous proof. The Brahman is beyond the reach of the eyes but by no means is it a negative concept, or an abstraction or a void. It is the essence of the knower. The world according to Sankara is *relatively* real (Vyavaharika Satya), while Brahman is *absolutely* real.The unchanging Brahman appears as the changing world through Maya or ignorance. To Sankara, the individual soul is only relatively real. It identifies itself with the body, mind and the senses, as long as it is deluded by ignorance. But In reality it is not different from Brahman or the Absolute.

The Upanishads declare emphatically: *Tat Tvam Asi* (That Thou Art). The Advaita philosophy of Sri Sankara is a system of bold philosophy and logical subtlety, coming from a genius and a profound thinker.

Visishtadvaita

Visishtadvaita is qualified non-dualism. Ramanujacharya through his commentary on Brahma Sutras is its best proponent. Visishtadvaita is aligned to Sri Vaishnava and is more of a philosophy of religion rather than an independent spiritual philosophy. Worship and spirituality are closely knit here.

While in the liberated state jiva is para, Jiva has consciousness in un-liberated state, unlike in Advaita where jiva is just a witness even in un-liberated state.There are three Tatvas (philosophical concepts): Isvara or Brahman, the independent reality; and Jiva and Prakriti, realities dependent on Brahman.

Moksha or liberation

Visishtadvaita does not accept the jivanmukti (liberation) concept of Advaita and holds that liberation is possible only after the jiva leaves the body. Moksha here is gradual and stepwise: reaching higher worlds like heaven, moving to still higher worlds and ultimately accomplishing oneness with God.

Moksha sadhana or resources for liberation

Apart from *Tatva* (discussed above), *hita* and *purushartha* are two more sadhanas (resources) for moksha. Hita comprises knowledge of five kinds: nature of self, nature of the eternal, fulfilment of the purpose or goal of life, paths to moksha, and obstacles in attainment of moksha.

Moksha upaya or methods of liberation

The paths to moksha are five: Karma (religious duty), Jnana (spiritual knowledge), Bhakti (devotion and worship), Prapatti (surrender) and acharyabhimana or faithful adherence to the teacher's words.

Guruji Golwalkar

Qn: Can we have a brief sketch of Sri Golwalkar?

Ans: Sri Golwalkar (full name Madhav Sadashiv Golwalkar) was affectionately called Guruji by his followers. Guruji became the chief of RSS after the demise of its founder Dr K B Hedgewar in 1940 and held the post till his demise in 1973. His original surname was Padhye. Padhye means a practicing priest. The Padhyes belong to an area known as Golwali. Out of the surname Golwalkar Padhye, only Golwalkar remained in due course.

Before becoming the Chief of RSS, Guruji spent a number of years in Ramakrishna Ashram. Swami Akhandananda, a direct disciple of Swami Vivekananda, was his spiritual Guru. He also served as Professor in Benaras Hindu University earlier.

He was a seer, thinker, organiser and an everlasting source of inspiration. His thoughts on various issues concerning Hindu Society are relevant even today. To know more about this great man, please go through a compilation of his thoughts, titled *'Bunch of thoughts',* which contains his resplendent vision of our nation, dimmed and almost lost through mental confusion and intellectual delusion over several centuries.

On a personal note: Despite his 24/7 schedule, Pujya Sri Guruji was regular in performing Sandhyavandana. I had the fortune of interacting with this great soul several times from 1964 to 1975 when I was actively associated with RSS, and receiving his blessings. I recollect one occasion when both the Acharyas of Kanchi, Sri Sri Maha Swamigal and Sri Sri Jayendra Saraswati Swamigal addressed and blessed the cadres at a training camp of RSS in Hyderabad in the year 1967.

Guruji was indeed a glorious personality.

On Conquering Fear

Qn. I realise fear plays havoc in one's life. How does one overcome fear ?

Ans. Yes, the main enemy of man is fear. We face many difficulties in life, a problem, an obstacle, or a disease. We can get over them either by seeking help from others, or through a palliative, or by taking medicine. Some difficulties even disappear on their own. But fearing a problem and its consequences aggrevates the situation and sometimes blockks a solution. For instance if bodily ailment is compounded with mental anguish caused by fear of "what will happen", the malady may worsen beyond cure. How do we present fear for overtaking the mind?

Come what may, with God's eternal Grace we will get over it; If this resolution is firmly anchored in our mind, there is no room for fear and we can manage any situation.

A certain stoicism and belief in praraabda karma also helps us get rid of fear. "I' m sufering the ill effects of myactions of earlierbirths. Let me invoke the Almighty's name, do my karmas and put up with these hardships and the best of my arbitrary" - This can be a great approach to overcome fear.

The problems we face pale into insignificance before the difficulties that great souls like Sri Rama, Harischandra, Bhakta Ramdas or the Pandavas faced. Even in the recent past, Mahatmas like Sri Ramakrishna, Ramana Maharshi, Guruji Gowalkar, Kanchi Peetadhipathi Sri Sri Jayendra Saraswati Swamigal and numerous great men have suffered. In a way we have to welcome the problems and consequent suffering as a means to expiate for the deeds done during our past karm but face up to it and weather the storms in our lives. It is not good to break down under adversity.

Prapta and Prarabdha

Qn. I am interested to know the distinction between Prapta and Prarabdha.

Ans. Prapta is what we deserve during the present life. Parabdham is what we experience because of deeds in our earlier births.

Both enjoin on us the importance of doing our duty with complete faith in God, as the only way to maintain our balance.

It is worthwhile quoting Kanchi Maha Swamigal's epic words here, on this subject:

The vicissitudes of a person's life are entirely attributable to his karmas and their results. One can seek pariharam for the consequences of karma through one's horoscope or by medicine or even mantras, but these will be effective only after the karma has spent its force. The real, unquestionable parihara is to lead life in total surrender to God with absolute devotion, accepting what we get from Him. One should develop this maturity – that's the true answer.

This will give us the ability to withstand previous karma impact and at the same time not to add on to our karma woes by our deeds in the present birth.

Azhwars

Qn. Please tell me about the Azhwars

Ans. The Azhwars, twelve in number, were characterized by boundless devotion to Lord Vishnu and profound knowledge and wisdom. The names of the 12 Azhwars are:

Poigai Azhwar
Bhoodatthu Azhwar
Pey Azhwar
Tirumazhisai Azhwar
Nammazhwar
Madhurakavi
Kulasekaran
Periyazhwar Andal
Thondar Adippodi
Tiruppaanazhwar
Tirumangai Azhwar

They have in all composed 24 'granthas' or treatises, comprising about 4,000 songs. A speciality of their writings is that four of these are considered on par with the 4 Vedas. Here is the comparison:

Tiruviruttam	Rig Veda
Tiru Asiriyam	Yajur Veda
Periya Tiruvandadi	Atharvana Veda
Tiruvaimozhi	Sama Veda

Here I like to present to the readers an Anugraha Bashana by the Kanchi Maha Swamigal which gives us an insight as to how the Vaishnavites view and prectice the Acharya tradition:

In Sri Ramanuja's tradition....

"Generally speaking, Srivaishnavites attach great importance to the quality of humility. The Srivaishnavite calls himself as a *dasa* when he meets someone. When he prostrates before others he uses the term *sevikkiren*. While he calls the elders of cults other than his own as swami, he calls the elder of his cult as "perumal".

Sri Vaishnavites recite with great fervour the episodes relating to their Guru parampara. Be it the temples dedicated to Lord Vishnu or Azhwars especially Andal, or the temples following thengalai tradition such as those for ManavaLa Ma MunigaL, Pillai Logachariar and others or the temples that follow vadagalai tradition such as one for Sri Vedanta Desika, see with what great religious fervour they conduct the aradhana! Even the Perumal, the Lord, here becomes secondary.

In many Vaishnavite temples we can also see the deities are installed and pujas conducted important personalities who came before and after Sri Ramanuja such as NadhamunihaL, Aalavandar, Manakkal Nambi, Tirukkachchi Nambi, Kuraththazhwan, Battar, Nanjeer and others. When compared to this tradition, we cannot claim that similar importance is given in Saivite temples to the Nayanmars, Maanikkavachakar and to those who propounded Saivite tenets (like Srikantacharyar, Meikantasivam and Umapathi Sivacharyar). It is almost nil also if we take the cases of great personalities who came before or after Sri Adi Sankara. In some rare cases, of course there are idols for Sri Adi Sankara (Acharya) especially in places in and around Kanchi and in temples at Mangadu and Tiruvotriyur. Generally speaking, if we take a census of all the temple idols and their worship as a scale to judge the influence of a siddhantha, then we may safely conclude that there is no such religious sect known as Advaita at all. And as I used to say, the reason for this is that the Advaitis are Smarthas while they preserve their separate idenity, accept only to a certain extent both Saivism and Vaishnavism. What I am arriving it is to emphasize the special devotion that the followers of Sri Ramanuja bestow on their religious leaders.

The devotion Sri Ramanuja's direct disciples had for him was unparalleled. They were even prepared to sacrifice their lives. One such disciples was Kurathazhwan. He belonged to a village called Kuram near Kanchipuram. You may remember that I have told you elsewhere that out of abundant bhakthi, Srivaishnavites who are otherwise well known for their polite language, as an exception, call Sri Vedanta Desikar as "Desikan", in singular. Similarly, they call Kurathazhwar as "Kurathazhwan". It may be noted that if Srivaishnavites mention Azhwan, it denotes only Kurathazhwan.

The King who ruled during Sri Ramanuja's period was a staunch saivite. At that time, Sri Ramanuja has been propagating the siddantha according to which only Lord Vishnu deserved to be worshipped and not Lord Shiva or other Devatas. The King desired to discuss this Ramanuja's assertion in a learned assembly. Gangaikonda Cholapuram was his capital then. The assembly was to congregate there and the King sent word to Sri Ramanuja to attend it. Sri Ramanuja was in Srirangam at that time. On seeing the retinue of the King, Kurathazhwar was greatly upset. It was then that Kurathazhwar decided to sacrifice everything including his life if necessary to save his Guru. He decided to adorn the saintly dress of his Guru and present himself as his Guru before the king. He fervently prayed and begged Sri Ramanuja that he be permitted to do this. "If there be any danger, let me face it alone." he said. Sri Ramanuja reluctantly agreed to this arrangement. Wearing a white dhoti, Sri Ramanuja departed from Chola empire to Melkottai (Thiru Narayanapuram) in Karnataka. This event is even now celebrated as a festival called vellai saathuppadi.

Meanwhile, Kurathazhwar wearing the *kaashaayam*, saintly dress, left for Gangaikonda Cholapuram where the learned assembly met. Kurathazhwan refused to accept the supremacy of Lord Siva and as anticipated was meted out the royal punishment. Only that he was not awarded death penalty but had to lose both his eyes. He accepted this punishment gladly feeling that his master had escaped this horror. He became totally blind. After the death of the king, Sri Ramanuja returned to Tamil Nadu in immense grief as his disciple had to lose his eyes for him.

Even though in later days Sri Ramanuja was living in Srirangam, he had resided in his earlier years in Kanchipuram where he was performing *theertha kainkaryam* to Sri Varadaraja Swami who was his *ishta devata*. Even as he was fully involved in arranging for the aradhana krama in Srirangam, he yet retained a soft corner towards Sri Varadaraja Swami of Kanchi. He hence asked Kurathazhwan to pray Lord Varadaraja to restore him his vision; if not for Kurathazhwan himself, but at least for his mental satisfaction. Obeying Guru's command, Kurathazhwan prayed to the Lord to restore his vision. In fact, he was least interested in having the eye sight restored.

He felt thus:" As per Sastric injunctions, one can get Iswara Darshan only if the sense organs are kept under control. In the guise of royal punishment in losing the vision we had the benefit of preventing at least one sense organ doing mischief. And what we really gain by getting it back, only to be drawn into the worldly affairs? But I have to obey the commands of my Acharya and should not let him grieve over me. Hence Oh! My Lord!! Kindly restore my vision for the limited purpose of having the darshan of my Acharya and Your Holy Self only." The Lord Varadaraja granted the boon.

Sri Madura Kavi was one of the Azhwars. He had actually composed only one *paasuram*, a eleven liner. Even though the *paasuram* is not on Lord Mahavishnu, it was still included in Naalayira Divya Prabhandam, and Sri Madura Kavi himself was raised to the status of an Azhwar. The reason is for his unique devotion towards his Guru, Sri Nammazwar, on whom the paasuram was sung. In the Ramanuja tradition, the Azhwars have the status as that of Acharyas. And even among them, Sri Nammazhwar has a special distinction of being called, 'Prappanna kootasthar'."

The Hindu Calender – God's time

Qn. Please explain the Hindu concept of time.

Ans. Kala (time) is a manifestation of God according to our Hindu theory of creation. The Kala chakra, the cycle of creation, is created by Him. *Srishti* and *Samhara,* creation and dissolution, are parts of this never-ending process in cyclic succession.The Hindu calendar can best be understood by the first part of the sankalpa with which we start every ritual, every formal puja. In this part we chant the details of the time period in which we live. This portion runs thus: *"Dwiteeya parardhe shweta varaha kalpe, vaivaswata manvantare, ashthavimsati tame, kaliyuge, prathame pade".*

Concept of Yuga: According to our Hindu cosmology, life in this universe is created and dissolved within each time-cycle or kala chakra. The cycle is never-ending: the end of one chakra is the beginning of the next. Yuga in Hindu philosophy is an important section of this chakra and constitutes an 'epoch' or 'era'. To equate God's time to man's time, look at this table:

1 Deva varsha = 360 human years

1 Chaturyuga, comprising Kaliyuga, Dwaparayuga, Tretayuga and Kritayuga = 12,000 deva varshas or 43.20 lakh human years

71 Chaturyugas	=	1 Manvantara
14 Manvantaras	=	1 Kalpa
2 Kalpas	=	Brahma's one day

A day for Brahma is therefore equal to 860 crore human years. A manvantara, which is roughly 30.67 crore human years, is the time the Sun takes to complete one revolution around the centre of the Milky Way. (I may add that we find there is some variations in calculations on the above between some puranas).

Incidentally we are now in the seventh manvantara, called 'Vaivasvata'. This year (2010 AD) is the Kali year 5111. Putting it another way, we are presently in the Kaliyuga of the 28th Mahayuaga of the 7th manvantara known as vaivasvata manvantara, of the Brahma's day.

SANKALPA (COMMITMENT) AND ITS MEANING

Qn. In all our rituals we begin the program with a sankalpa – a commitment or resolution – to the devata (God) who is being worshipped. We chant these words starting *"Shubhe shobhane muhurte…."* mindlessly and often incorrectly. It will help if you could tell us what this sankalpa is, and why we chant it.

Ans. The sankalpa, which as you say is chanted in all pujas and other rituals at the start, comprises four sections interwoven seamlessly, to announce four important things:

- Which time-cycle am I presently in – the unique Hindu concept of Yuga
- Where am I doing this ritual – a description of the geography
- On which day and at what time am I doing it – the precise tithi and nakshatra and
- What will be I be doing in the course of this ritual?

The first part starting with *'shubhe shobhane muhurte'* and ending with *'pratame paade'* sets out the details of the time-cycle in which we live, called Yuga. Yuga can be roughly equated to an era or an age within the kala chakra or the overall time cycle. The Hindu concept of time is cyclical and not linear. This cycle of creation is God's work.

Srishti and *Samhara,* creation and dissolution, are the two parts of this never-ending process in a long cyclic succession of events.

(An explanation of this concept is given in an answer to the previous question on the Hindu concept of time.)

The second section, starting with *'jumbudweepe'* and ending with *'vyavaharike'* takes one through the geography: it describes the setting of the place from which the person is taking the sankalpa. In essence this talks of Bharata or India, the motherland of the Hindus, and our coordinates and boundaries.

The Sankalpa starts with "Adhya Brhmanaha, Dwitiya Parardhe, Sweta varaha kalpe, Vaivasvata manvantare, Ashtavimsati tame, Kali yuge…. "

- *Adhya Brahmanaha* literally means that the person who does the Sankalpa starts from Brahma's life.
- *Dwitiya Parardha* means Brahma's second Parardha. One Parardha consists of 50 Brahma years. Now the second Parardha is running.
- *Sweta Varaha Kalpa* is the first of the thirty Kalpas according to Matsya Purana.
- *Vaivasvata manvantra:* There are fourteen manvantras in a Kalpa, and the present one is seventh and its name is Vaivasvata manvantra.
- *Ashtavimsati tama* means 18,000 Kalpas has been now completed.
- *Kaliyuge-Prathame pade* means we are in the first quarter of the Kaliyuga.
- *Jambu Dweepe, Bharata Varshe, Bharata Khande* describes the geographical area of our motherland.

The third part of the sankalpa focuses on the specific date and time of the ritual. Starting with the schema of 60 years *('Prabhavadi sashtya samvatsaranam madhye")*, it specifies the year, the month, the paksha, the day (vasara), the date (tithi), and the nakshatra.

The other terminologies that we come across in our sankalpa are:

The Varsha: There are 60 years in a cycle and each year (Samvatsara) has a name. The name of the current year is Vikruti (2010-11).

The Ayana: There are two ayanas in a year viz., Uttarayana (roughly January to June) and Dakshinayana (roughly July to December). Each ayana has a period of six months.

The Ritu: There are six Ritus (seasons) in a year, viz., (i) Vasanta (ii) Greeshma (iii) Varsha (iv) Sharat (v) Hemanta (vi) Shishira.

The Masa: There are twelve months in a year. They are Mesha, Vrushabha, Mituna, Kataka, Simha, Kanya, Tula, Vrichika, Dhanur, Makara, Kumbha, and Meena.

The Paksha: A paksha consists of 15 days and two pakshas make a month. Shukla paksha starts the day after amavasya and ends with pournami. Krishna paksha starts the day after pournami and ends with amavasya.

The Tithi: Every day has a tithi and in a paksha we have 15 such tithis. The same set will appear in both the Shukla and Krishna pakshas. These are the ordinal numbers of the days.

The Vasara: Sunday (Bhanu vasara), Monday (Indu vasara), Tuesday (Bhauma vasara), Wednesday (Sowmya vasara), Thursday (Guru vasara), Friday (Brugu vasara) and Saturday (Sthira vasara) are the seven days of the week.

The Nakshatra: The Hindu calendar has 27 nakshatras during each month, repeated 12 times in a year. The name of the nakshtra of the day is announced as part of the sankalpa.

Finally, the actual resolve or commitment is chanted: *"asmakam sakutumbhanam kshema..."* concluding with *"karishye"* (I shall do). The karta spells out the purpose of the puja or the ritual, the God or Goddess for whom it is done, and the benefits being sought in terms of the health, wealth etc. of the family of the karta.

Sri Sri Jayendra Saraswathi Swamigal

Qn. Aren't sanyasis supposed to have relinquished everything temporal and dedicate themselves totally to worship? From this standpoint, how proper is the involvement of Sri Sri Jayendra Saraswati Swamigal, in social causes and his voicing of opinions on national issues and public matters?

Ans. We have no authority or qualification to comment on the actions of our Guru, the Head of our religion. Our job is to seek Guru kataksha (the blessings of the Guru) unquestioningly and with no doubt about what he is doing. Let us do our job, with the confidence that he is doing what he is ordained to do. This is needless confusion with matters that do not concern us.

Let me quote Kanchi Maha Swamigal on this subject, from his 'Deivaththin Kural' (Vanathi Publishers).

"There are four types of Sanyasis: *kuteechaka, baheetaka, hamsa* and *paramahamsa.* Advaita sanyasis belong to the fourth variety i.e. Paramahamsa. These swamis, who belong to the Adi Sankara Bhagavad Pada mutts, occupy the peetha of the mutt for an important responsibility viz. expounding the dharmas to ordinary people of the religion The paramahamsa sanyasi cannot be totally devoid of any contact with humanity and be only in the perennial quest of God. He has the office job of communicating religion and its manuals to people in the other ashrams and administrate the math to which he belongs. To this extent, therefore, some changes in his day to day life are inevitable".

We should consider ourselves fortunate that we are living at the time of Sri Sri Jayendra Swamigal and getting direct advice from him on the conduct of our lives according to Hindu dharma.

One cannot question the wisdom of Maha Swamigal in selecting Sri Sri Jayendra Saraswati Swamigal as his successor.

Equally, one has no business questioning the acts of our Acharyal. It is my unshakeable belief that what he is doing is in consonance with the Yuga Dharma and that we should follow in his footsteps without doubt or confusion.

Sri Sri Jayendra Swamigal has traversed the length and breadth of India – **entirely by foot** – three times - with social consciousness and keeping in mind the variegated society of India today. He has moved with people of all languages and regions and spoken to them in their tongue in his task of propagating Hindu dharma across the nation.

We know very little about the life of this great, multifaceted personality. His experience, his work and his approach have several dimensions: religious, spiritual, ritualistic, Vedic, knowledge-oriented – and worldly. Each one of these dimensions has a meaning and a purpose.

Let us look at just one example. This is from the book Tamizh Maalai by Dr. R Nagaswami, renowned archaeologist and a friend of mine. I quote from P. 125. "I had the great fortune of getting the darshan of Sri Sri Jayendra Saraswati Swamigal in Chennai, at Valasaravakkam. I showed him a rare volume 'Bala bedam' of a legendary writer who lived in Tanjavur centuries ago, who was an expert on Advaita and at home in both Tamil and Sanskrit. The moment I showed the book to him the Swamigal said at once with a smile 'yes, I know Sri Kuppuswami has authored not only this particular one but several others'. He gave me further information about the great author".

Dr Nagaswamy continues: He must be omniscient – that can be the only explanation. It also showed that Swamigal had a marvellous memory, beautifully indexed, which could get him to respond instantly to the mention of a little-known fact. What he said next floored me. He said "you must microfilm this and make it into a CD. We cannot afford to lose this precious gift. I came out from the darshan full of awe and wonder. *(Incidentally Sri Kuppusamy belongs to a caste in Tamil Nadu known as Vellalar).*

Readers will recall many such incidents proclaiming the immense reach of Sri Sri Jayendra Saraswati Swamigal and proving that he is no less than a Mahatma.

To recapitulate, the Sri Mutts of Bhagavad Padal have been established for a specific purpose, of propagating our religion. So the sanyasi who heads the Mutts and other Sanyasis who belong to the Mutts are not ordinary sanyasis who can be content with japa and tapa. Their approach and actions have to be in sync with the Yuga dharma of the particular period. And it has always been that way, over the centuries. It is no different now. If we understand and appreciate this truth, things become clear and simple.

****

THE GLORY OF DARBHAI

Darbhai, also called kusa, is a grass leaf and its role and place in a Brahmin's life is supreme. Darbhai is considered as a form of wealth and can cleanse us of our sins as it has the power to purify. We must have at least basic knowledge about this holy grass leaf, and that is the purpose of this monograph.

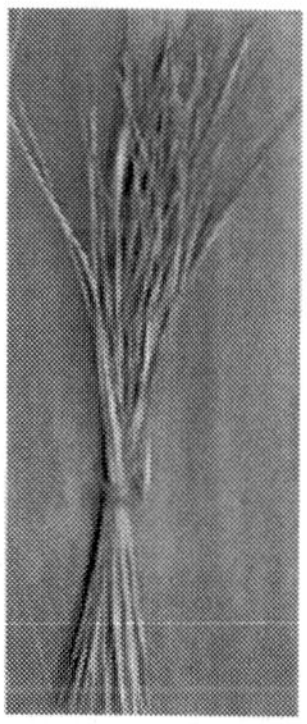
Darbhai

There are several types of grass that can be used such as darbhai, viswamitra, kusa, munja, sara, doorva etc. The botanical name of darbhai is Poa Cynosuroides. Even modern researchers speak of its special characteristics and the power of its vibrations.

Tradition avers that Brahma resides at the roots of kusa, Kesava in the centre and Sankara in the tip; and other Gods in the four directions - as in the case of a peepal tree.

Great sages like Harita, Markandeya, Atri, Kausika, Vyasa, Saataatapa, Yajnavalkya, Asvalayana and Apasthamba have eulogized darbhai. Though there are minor variations in the use of darbhai in deva karmas and pitru karmas, there is unison among all the Rishis in underscoring the place of darbhai in all rites and rituals.

The Vedas too speak specifically of the value of darbhai: the acchidra section of Krisnayajurveda Braahmama is a case in point.

Reference to darbhai is found in granthas, the ancient texts of Sara-samuchaya, Smrti-saram, Smrti-ratnam, Smrti chintamani, Smrti-bbaskara and Vishnupurana. There are many Puranic stories woven around darbhai. The Mahabharata contains the story of Garuda, the mythic bird and Vishnu's vehicle bringing ambrosia and the serpents getting their tongue split lengthwise when they licked the darbha leaf on which a few drops of the ambrosia fell. The story of Rama throwing darbhai at Jayanta in the shape of a crow can be found in the Ramayana. In the story of Mahabali Vamana clears the spout of pitcher with a leaf of darbhai.

How to wear the 'Pavitram'

The darbhai is to be worn on the ring finger of the right hand, in a circular formation, prior to starting any religious rite like homa, dana, yaga-yagna – in fact any deva or pitru karma. This ubiquitous adornment on the finger of the karta of any ritual is called a 'pavitram', and it is necessarily made of darbhai.

There is an opinion that one can permanently have the 'pavitram' on. Perhaps an extension of this thinking is the idea ascribed to sages like Katyayana and Harita that a pavitram could be made of gold and worn all the time. Please note that a pavitram made of gold cannot substitute a darbhai. When a karma starts one has to necessarily have a darbhai pavitram on, even if one is already wearing a swarna pavitram. Any reference to pavitram means only darbhai.

Incidentally, when a swarna pavitram is worn on the ring finger, a ring called tarjani made of silver is to be simultaneously worn on the index finger. And only the eldest son can wear the tarjani (but not when his father is alive).

Generally one does not prepare darbhai for oneself. It is either received from the family Purohit (Sastrigal) or a properly qualified elderly person. Of course if the pavitram is not available from these sources one can prepare it oneself. The darbhai has to be fresh and prepared just before the start of a ritual – it should not be stocked.

There are restrictions in the number of darbha leaves used to prepare the pavitram. In Vedic recitations, meditation and for puja it is prepared from 2 leaves of the grass. In all ancestral worship like Sraaddha or Amavasya libations we use 3 leaves. In death rites darbhai is prepared with one leaf of the grass. Though the number of leaves may change, the shape, size and method of preparing it do not change.

As we have already seen, there are quite a few options for the leaf to be used as darbhai. The type known as viswamitra is available in plenty. Other grass leaves like that of paddy, wheat, yava, rundhura, and usiram (vlamicheri ver) can also be used.

Regulations for wearing & discarding the pavitram

The karta should first do aachamana while taking the pavitram from his acharya, preparatory to the start of the ritual. Likewise, the performance should end with an aachamana.

On both occasions (i.e. when aachamana is done), the pavitram is to be positioned over the right earlobe. At the commencement the karta will do the aachamana, take the pavitram from the ear and wear it on his finger as described above. At the conclusion of the rite, he has to remove the pavitram from the ear, untie it and throw it in the niruriti (south-west) direction and do the aachamana.

If the karta has to drink water during the ritual or sip milk etc. as part of the ceremony, he should not drink with the pavitram on. He should lodge it over the right earlobe and drink.

The pavitram should not be kept elsewhere or handed over to anyone.

Similarly while doing paada prakshalana (a ritual of washing another person's feet) the pavitram must be removed from the finger and placed above the right earlobe.

Use of darbhai grass other than as pavitram

- It becomes the asana or seat for doing Vedic karmas.
- It serves as a connecting link between husband and wife during a ritual when they do sankalpa (take a resolve to do the karma). The wife touches her husband with darbhai grass.
- At the time of temple consecration (kumbabhishekam) the kalasa is connected to the idol and the tower with a rope made of darbha grass (Nadisandama).
- Darbhai is believed to protect food prepared during an eclipse.
- Darbhai is a must in all homas (in places like Paristheeriya, paatra sadhana, ayaamita, aajya samskara, etc.)

- Along with the mango leaves and coconut, a koorcham made of darbhai is also placed in the kalasa where avahana is performed for devas.

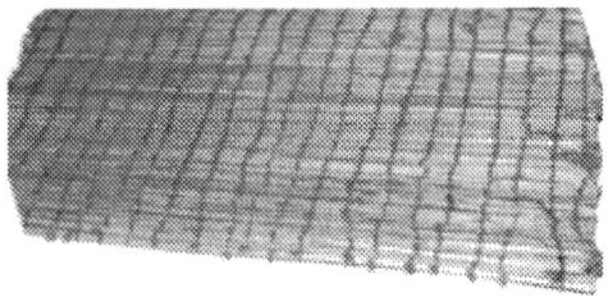

- A belt made of darbhai grass is tied around the waist of the brahmachari during upanayana, and around the waist of the bride in a marriage.
- For brahmavarana (the selectionof a vidwans or scholar) in homas, darbhai is used.
- A small clutch of darbhai is handed over to the acharya to whom power of attorney is given by the karta with a request that the acharya may perform the proposed japa or homa on his behalf.

Do's and don'ts

The tip of the darbhai should be intact. The grass leaf without the tip is useless.

When we take darbhai from a bundle, we have to do it from the lower/root side and not from the top.

When we set it down, care must be taken to see that its tip faces east or north.

The darbhai should not be placed on bare earth.

Darbhai cannot be reused; or and if it is trampled it should not be used again.

Darbhai grass should not be cut with our nails.

Summary

Darbhai purifies us, protects us from any mishaps during the ritual. Harita Maharishi emphatically says the merit of rituals done with pavitram becomes manifold. To quote another sage, "pavitram is like the Vajrayudha in the hands of Indra, the Trisula in the hands of Siva, Chakra in the hands of Vishnu. All bad and negative forces like demons etc. run away once they see a pavitram-paani, the hand that wears a pavitram."

So in future when you receive a pavitram from the Acharya, do please keep in mind its value and greatness and don't treat it as a mere grass-leaf.

****

ARYA-DRAVIDA RACE THEORY

The very first page of our school History textbook begins with the Aryan invasion of India. The Aryans are supposed to have driven away the original inhabitants of India to remote mountain corners and taken possession of the country. We are told further that our country has a history of a series of successive foreign invasions, and Indian culture is therefore only a medley of the cultures of invaders. Influenced perhaps by the Western theory our leaders also describe India as a 'nation in the making'. This self-deprecating view is entirely untrue.

The genesis of this theory

During the medieval Ages the Portuguese, the Dutch, the French and the British came to India to seek business opportunities. The astute British prevailed, because they discovered and exploited our weaknesses. They called our land a subcontinent i.e., a mixture of several cultures. To establish their supremacy over the entire land, they sold the idea to everyone that Hindus had never stayed together as a single nation. This helped them initiate religious conversions as well.

The core of the British strategy was the policy of 'divide & rule' and propagation of the Arya Dravida race theory. Their campaign was so convincing that even Indian intellectuals and historians accepted it meekly.

Sir W. Turner, Sir H. Risley, Dr. W.W. Hunter, Dr. Greersan, J.C. Rhode, H.G. Wells, Dr. Kaene, Edward Thomas and Bishop Caldwell are some of the Europeans who generated different race theories, all with the conclusion that the original homeland of Aryans was outside India. It is regrettable that long after freeing our country from British rule we still cling to these prejudiced race theories as gospel truth.

The word 'Arya' has nothing to do with the 'Aryan' coined by Western scholars in the last century and a half. The term used in Vedic literature is a qualitative one, with absolutely no racial overtones. The word 'Arya' occurs about forty times in the Rig Veda and nowhere is the word used to designate a race.

Dr. B.R. Ambedkar has treated the subject elaborately in one of his books 'Who are the shudras?' He concludes that the Aryan Race theory set up by the western writers falls to the ground for its sheer lack of logic.

Firstly the theory is based on assumptions and inferences from the assumptions. Secondly it is a perversion of scientific investigation: a hypothesis is preconceived and facts are conveniently strung together to prove it. There is no evidence in the Vedas of any invasion of India by the Aryan race and their conquest over the Dasas and Dasyus (supposed to be natives of India).

The original homeland of the Aryans has been variously stated to be Central Asia, the Volga valley, Scandinavia Baltic regions, Southern Russia, Siberia, the Northwestern Kirghiz Steppes and Central Germany by different scholars – there is neither unanimity nor proof. We can only conclude from this that the whole theory of extraneous origin of Aryans is only an unfounded conjecture.

K.A. Nilakanta Sastri notes in his book 'Advanced History of India' (Page 32) that the latest edition of 'Oxford History of India' has omitted discussion concerning the original home of the Aryans because no hypothesis seems to be finally established.

Another argument that Aryans originally belonged to the Arctic region also stands on no firm ground. Our ancestors probably lived in that region – they could have even lived there for a long while before returning to their homeland.

This view is emphatically endorsed by Sri. Balasastry Hardas, a historian & Sanskrit scholar, in his book 'Glimpses of the Vedic Nation'. He says: "It is perfectly right to raise a question why the Aryans who had gone to the Arctic region abandoned their colonies and returned to their Homeland. The answer is not hard to imagine: we have many instances in history of a particular conquering race abandoning its conquered countries and releasing its grip over the subdued people. The causes for such an occurrence are indeed many and multifarious. The Romans who had held England under their sway had to return (for instance) because of difficulties, disorders and dangers in their own homeland."

Original home of Aryans - India

But there is ample evidence to show that India was the original home of Aryans and that any strains of Indian culture found elsewhere were taken out of Bharat. There is nothing in our ancient Vedic literature to substantiate their migration to India. None of the sages have ever talked about conquests by a migrated race.

Would a migrated race praise Bharat as their mother, consider the Himalayas as the abode of their God, and rivers Ganga and Kaveri as sacred? Generally an invading race would boast its achievements - do we have instances of such show-off?

Prof. T. Burrow in 'The Sanskrit Language' asserts the following: "For the Indo-Aryan invasion of India no direct evidence is available... in the text of the Rig Veda itself although historical allusions are not uncommon; there is no reference anywhere to the fact of the migration, nor any definite indication that it was still remembered."

Was India a Dravidian homeland?

The theory of India being Dravidian Homeland should be dismissed as a contrivance to establish the theory of Aryans being invaders and effect a divide between the two races. Bishop Caldwell has stated, in a different context, that Dravidians also entered India through the Northwest. That means the original inhabitants of this ancient land were neither Aryans nor Dravidians - this is patently absurd.

Ancient Tamil texts like Manimekalai, Paripadal etc. indicate cultural oneness of the Dravidians with the rest of Hindus. Whatever is hypothetically presumed to be Dravidian turns out, after proper scrutiny, to be nothing but Hindu.

The monumental volume 'Mohenjo-Daro & Indus Valley Civilisation' prepared by Sir J. Marshall, the then Director of Archaeology (Government of India) states that the diggings do not convince one of a whole and complete civilisation: it is only a representation or a part of a great one. He also asserts that the finds do not have any great resemblance with the alleged Sumerian culture. He observes: "Points of difference between these civilisations are more numerous than the points of similarity" (Times of India, 28th Jan 1929).

The words 'Arya & Dravida'

The words Arya and Dravida are part of the Sanskrit lexicon and their meanings can be derived conclusively only from Sanskrit texts and dictionaries. In Sanskrit the word 'Arya' means worthy, noble, respectable, dignified etc. It can therefore be inferred that one can be called 'Aryan' if one possesses the qualities cited. Several anecdotes can be quoted from Ramayana and Mahabharata to substantiate this.

Indian society enjoys the incessant flow of Sanatana Dharma, the eternal religion, through the length and breadth of this sacred land. The seeming variations are at best sporadic. The Vedas, Upanishads, Ramayana and Mahabharata belong to the land and are held in high esteem and veneration. The basic beliefs and traditions remain the same throughout the land. Such commonness of philosophy can hardly be ascribed to invading cultures. It is a matter of shame, therefore, that we believe the theory and pass it on to posterity.

Swami Vivekananda has condemned this attitude outright in the following words: "And what your European pundits say about the

Aryans swooping down from some foreign land, snatching away the lands of the aborigines and settling in India by exterminating them, is all pure nonsense, foolish talk. Strange, that our India Scholars too say 'Amen' to them and all these monstrous lies are being taught to our boys! This is very bad indeed. In what Veda, in what Sukta do you find that the Aryans came to India from a foreign country?" ('The East & the West' - Page 94).

In conclusion

At no time did any division exist in our society of two distinctive races as Aryans and Dravidians. We do not dispute the existence of several kingdoms in this land, but this in no way contradicts the essential oneness of the nation. And it is baseless to say that an independent and exclusive 'Dravidian' civilisation opposed to the Vedic Dharma existed at any point of time. Let us give the lie to this motivated theory and learn to live united under the single umbrella of our Hindu tradition.

****

THE TWILIGHT YEARS - GET BACK ON TRACK

A retired Brahmin usually spends time reading the newspaper, watching TV, taking grandchildren to school and occasionally going to the temple. Most retirees who go through this routine are reasonably happy with it and consider it ideal – is it?

Brahmin not by birth alone: A person born in the *dwijanma* class does not automatically get the Brahmin stamp: he has to earn it. He has to discover and reconfirm his identity through certain acts. One is born a Brahmin after many lives in different jiva-rasis. The birth as a Brahmin enjoins on him the responsibility to lead a life worthy of a Brahmin, failing which he probably gets back to lower jiva-rasis and has to start afresh.

We often speak proudly of our grandfather or great grandfather and their adherence to our culture. Do we come across our selves as role models to our own grandchildren? If not, isn't it time we did?

During our service period or as a business person, many of us do very well: we show great attitude, total integrity and loyalty to our chosen profession, and even set great paths for our next generation to follow. But the purpose of our birth, the rare birth as a Brahmin, is not just wearing a poonal, going to temples, offering charities and being good to fellow-citizens. It's much more.

The right start: During a Brahmin's 'earning' period he could be excused for ignoring his religious duties. But a retired person is hopefully free to spend time as he wishes: this is indeed the time to recover what he has lost so far in terms of his Brahmin identity.

Except for economic compulsions, the Brahmin should cease his pursuit of the Mammon immediately on retirement. He should not seek extension of his services but instead concentrate on the daily observances required of him by the scriptures, the Sastras. What are these?

Religious acts:

- Perform daily nitya karmas such as Sandhyavandana and puja
- Chant Gayatri mantra 1008 times daily (Gayatri japa)
- Perform Panchayatana puja or Salagrama aradhana daily
- Perform Aupasana daily if you have the facility at home

Physical changes:

- Grow a tuft, which is a Brahmin's distinct hallmark and which you had to forgo because of work and society-related, often imagined, compulsions.
- Avoid self shaving
- Do away with the moustache if you have grown one.
- Always wear the panchakachcham, again a distinct identity of a Brahmin.
- Never be seen wearing a single item like only the dhoti: your dress should include an uttareeya or a top – in other words the dress must have at least two pieces

Changes in habits and practices:

- Have the position of the poonal changed doing ablutions and wash the mouth and legs thereafter, as per the rules
- Pay more attention to sanctity, and things such as ' madi' and 'achara'
- Spare a significant chunk of time for some kind of public service
- Seek the guidance of a Guru to develop spiritual thinking

The lists above are illustrative and not exhaustive. You will get more ideas in due course, on your own. Put them into practice, with due directions from your Guru.

Gurus & pseudo persons: Preceptors who seek to educate common folk come in all hues – yogis, babas, anandas, gurujis etc. How does one know if the guru one has sought is genuine? The selection of a proper acharya calls for great care and vigilance.

We can listen to discourses and follow ideas given by any sage – as long as we do not neglect the daily observances, the nitya karmas. A 'guru' who asks you to discontinue all pujas and be at his beck and call is more likely to be a charlatan than a genuine coach. It is sad to see some people coming under the influence of the wrong persons and not performing even Siva puja or Salagrama aradhana.

Our ancestors did not have this problem as they did not pay attention to anything other than what their own Mutts said. There were Siddha Purushas in those days too: and our elders respected them and took their guidance, but not at the cost of neglecting the tradition. In fact Siddha Purushas also encouraged adherence to those values. But the present day picture is different and we need to be on our guard.

What will help us steer clear of such misguiding guides is the unswerving practice of karmas we are ordained to do:

- Start doing Sandhyavandana at the scheduled hours daily. Learn it properly from your Purohit: he will be glad to teach you.
- Remember that Panchakachcham is not a uniform to be worn only by Purohits – it is your prescribed dress as well.
- Go to temple regularly
- Offer Namaskara to your Guru chanting 'abhivadaye', wherever you happent to see him.
- Shed your shyness, your fear of being laughed at – this change is important for you to evolve as a Brahmin and it doesn't matter if you are being commented upon. To be honest, no one has the time to look at you and pass remarks.

- Set up schedules to learn Suktas and Vedas, and in general keep adding to your religious repertoire and routine.
- Some have the concern that these acts looks like flaunting your Brahminism - far from it! As long as you don't do it for public appreciation but only because you are required to do it, you don't have to worry.

Sri Sri Chandrasekharendra Saraswati Swamigal:

Our cultural values and ritualistic processes are glorious. Let us not tire of these, but instead let us seek them in our retired life as a Godsend and shape our life accordingly. Retirement is not the time for tiring of Brahminism but achieving it. The following extract of an Anugraha Bhashana by Kanchi Acharya is very relevant in this regard.

"I have been telling you about many rituals that are to be followed. You may worry yourself that you can perform only some of these. Don't worry: do whatever is feasible, but do them regularly and diligently. And keep egging your mind about the ones you have left out. The mind will find a way to get you to do those as well."

****

Mangalani bhavantu